# HYPATIA
*of*
# ALEXANDRIA

# HYPATIA
*of*
# ALEXANDRIA
*Mathematician and Martyr*

MICHAEL A. B. DEAKIN

**Prometheus Books**
59 John Glenn Drive
Amherst, New York 14228-2197

Published 2007 by Prometheus Books

Inquiries should be addressed to
Prometheus Books
59 John Glenn Drive
Amherst, New York 14228–2197
VOICE: 716–691–0133, ext. 207
FAX: 716–564–2711
WWW.PROMETHEUSBOOKS.COM

11  10  09  08  07      5  4  3  2  1

Library of Congress Cataloging-in-Publication Data

Deakin, Michael A. B.
    Hypatia of Alexandria : mathematician and martyr / Michael A. B. Deakin.
        p. cm.
    Includes bibliographical references and index.
    ISBN 978–1–59102–520–7
    Hypatia, d. 415. 2. Mathematicians—Egypt—Biography. 3. Women mathematicians—Egypt—Biography. 4. Philosophers—Egypt—Biography. 5. Women philosophers—Egypt—Biography. 6. Alexandrian school. I. Title.

QA29.H88D43 2007
510.92—dc22
[B]                                                                          2007001588

Printed in the United States on acid-free paper

*The Virgin's starry Sign when e'er I see,*
*Adoring, on thy works I think and thee:*
*For all thy vertuous Works celestial are,*
*As are thy learned Words beyond compare,*
*Divine Hypatia, who dost far and near*
*Virtue's and Learning's spotless Star appear.*

# CONTENTS

# ACKNOWLEDGMENTS

*J* am grateful to a number of people who have helped me in important ways. Winifred Frost provided translations from the Greek and some of her contributions appear here, especially in appendixes B and D. But her guidance also informs many of the other parts of this book as well. Monty Wilkinson supplied much of the translation from Asmus's German that appears in appendix D, and both he and Hans Lausch have made clear to me matters that eluded my own meager grasp of German. Ivor Grattan-Guinness opened many doors for me when I paid an all-too-brief visit to London in pursuance of this research. Robert Penella has also greatly helped me in making available to me the relevant passages from Zintzen's work and in drawing to my attention the parallel researches of Maria Dzielska. Edith Mendez likewise supplied me with material unavailable in Australia. Peter Grossman pointed out a number of errors in an earlier draft. Some aspects of the mathematical exposition have benefited from discussions with my colleague John Stillwell. The sections on diophantine analysis were greatly improved by correspondence with Alf van der Poorten and Joseph L. Wetherell. Howard Landman and his Web site have been most valuable to me. Mick Fuller's computer expertise enabled the retrieval of files following the terminal breakdown of the machine where they were once stored.

This book expands a technical paper, published in the *American Mathematical Monthly*. I repeat my thanks to the persons acknowledged there: Winifred Frost (again) and Garry Tee. Several correspondents, in response to the publication of this account, have greatly assisted me, and I mention in particular the late David Fowler, the late Wilbur Knorr, Jacques Sesiano, and Donald Viney.

The sections on the "Hydroscope" owe much to the coauthor of the relevant technical paper, the late Charles Hunter, and I also take this opportunity to thank once again the late Peter Bicknell and Roger Shiner in connection with this aspect of the work.

The photographs are the work of Steve Morton and the diagrams were drawn by Jean Sheldon. The astrolabe in Plates 2 and 3 is described as: "Issued and Authenticated by the [US] National Maritime Historical Society [and] Crafted by the  Franklin Mint." It would seem to be modeled on an instrument described on pages 21-23 of *The Planispheric Astrolabe* (Greenwich National Maritime Museum, 1979).

My thanks also to Robin Turner for the loan of his astrolabe.

# A NOTE ON SPELLING CONVENTIONS

*T*he spelling conventions adopted here have been chosen to accord with common usage and for as much consistency as can reasonably be achieved. Thus, latinized forms have been employed in the main. Although Pappus should more accurately be transliterated from the Greek as Pappos, the former spelling is almost universal, and is in particular that adopted by the *Dictionary of Scientific Biography*. For this reason I have chosen to use such a convention throughout. There is currently something of a reaction to this; modern scholarship, for example, tends to prefer *Synesios* to *Synesius*, and, given that the man himself spoke no Latin, this makes a lot of sense. In other contexts, I have myself gone in this direction. Here, however, I have opted for consistency, and it remains true that much of the literature still employs the Latinate forms: *Synesius*, *Paeonius*, and so forth.

Similarly, I have accepted traditional transliterations involving the use of a *c* rather than a *k*. Thus I have used the spelling *Damascius*, and not *Damaskios*, and have *Canon* rather than *Kanon*, and so forth.

In one instance, however, I have felt compelled to adopt another convention. The English names of saints like *Cyril* are so widely accepted that it would be quite artificial not to use them, even if this does constitute a (formal) inconsistency.

When it comes to the names of books and other works, where there is an accepted English name, for example, the *Arithmetic*, I have used it. Where a non-English name has achieved wide currency

11

(e.g., the *Almagest* or the *Planisphaerium*) then I have used that. In certain cases, I have simply used what I think of as the standard title (e.g., *De Dono Astrolabii*). In this area, it would be pedantic to seek consistency.

In appendix B, I have retained Winifred Frost's spelling in her article reprinted there, even though its conventions are in places different from those of the rest of this book. Similarly, where in appendix D I rely on the translations of others, I have retained their spelling.

# INTRODUCTION

*I*magine a time when the world's greatest living mathematician was a woman, indeed, a physically beautiful woman, and a woman who was simultaneously the world's leading astronomer.

Imagine that she conducted her life and her professional work in a city as turbulent and troubled as Ayodhya or Amritsar, Baghdad or Beirut is today.

Imagine such a female mathematician achieving fame not only in her specialist field, but also as a philosopher and a religious thinker who attracted a large popular following.

Imagine her as a virgin martyr killed not *for* her Christianity, but *by* Christians because she was not one of them.

And imagine that the guilt of her death was widely whispered to lie at the door of one of Christianity's most honored and significant saints.

Would we not expect to have heard of all this? Would it not be shouted from the rooftops? Would it not be possible to walk into any bookstore and buy a biography of this woman? Would not her life be common knowledge?

You would think so, but such is not the case. And that is the reason for this book.

For Hypatia of Alexandria was indeed, at the time she was killed by Christian fanatics, the world's foremost mathematician and astronomer and also a leading Neoplatonic philosopher. Physically beautiful, devotedly celibate, she was the revered teacher of a man (Synesius of Cyrene) who, subsequently converted to Christianity, helped formulate the Christian doctrine of the Trinity, using Neoplatonic principles learned at her feet.

And yes, the shadow of guilt over her lynch-murder still clouds the memory of Saint Cyril of Alexandria, Doctor of the Universal Church, and, in particular, Doctor of the Incarnation.

But until quite recently you couldn't find easy access to a biography of her, let alone a reliable one.

Her name is, of course, invoked. For example, it has been given to not just one but two journals of feminist philosophy, as well as to an earlier feminist tract (by Dora Russell, the second wife of Bertrand Russell, the philosopher-mathematician). Gibbon, in his *Decline and Fall*, gave a particularly vivid account of her death; it is couched in the sparse rhetorical prose for which he is so justly admired: "In the bloom of beauty, and in the maturity of wisdom, the modest maid refused her lovers and instructed her disciples."

There are, to be sure, accounts of her life to be had and of these some are readily available and in English. But almost all of those that satisfy even one, let alone both, of these conditions are of extremely poor quality. This is unfortunately true even in those cases where we have every right to expect better.

This then is why I have written this book. I hope that it will say more of Hypatia, say it more clearly, say it more authoritatively, and say it more completely than any other such account available.

In particular, it will be the first book-length biography to attempt an evaluation of Hypatia's mathematics. In fact, it will be the first ever full-scale attempt to evaluate her mathematics.

Naturally there are available specialist accounts of different aspects of Hypatia's mathematical work. They are not readily accessible to the lay reader (and in all too many cases not very readily accessible to anyone). What is offered here is a synthesis—a collection between two covers of the different things we can say of Hypatia's life, times, and work.

However, I have had to compromise. One imagines that Hypatia herself would have seen a knowledge of mathematics as an integral part of an education. It would be nice to be able to think that in sixteen hundred subsequent years such a wish might have come to pass: nice to wish—impossible, in fact, to assume such knowledge from one's readers. Here I have presented enough of Hypatia's mathematics in the body of the text as I feel confident of discussing in nontechnical terms, such that I hope to carry my readers with me, but there are points where this is clearly not an option.

So in presenting Hypatia's achievement I have felt compelled to confine most of the technical details to the first of the appendixes, appendix A. This is, as I have said, a compromise, but one which is sanctioned by custom. If you, the reader, want the details, then they are there; if you can do without them, or are put off by them, then the relevant passage comes all of a piece as an easily skippable chunk.

I recall one of my early lectures on the subject; when I put an equation (a very simple one) on the board, I lost a significant part of my audience. Such is innumeracy today—or rather mathophobia as the symptom has been called. Regrettably, it's a fact, and a long-standing one at that.

There have been several biographies of Hypatia (those of book length being predominantly in German), but they nearly all skirt round her mathematics—this despite the primary sources all attesting to the fact that her greatest achievements lay in this field.

This seems to my view to omit the very core of the story. It is like writing of Goethe without analysing *Faust*, or of Omar Khayyám without the *Rubái'yat*, but in Hypatia's case it is the rule. There are more words to be read in fact on her philosophy, about which we know very little, than on her mathematics, about which we know quite a lot (incomplete though that knowledge may be).

The history of mathematics includes very few women prior to the twentieth century, and even today mathematics is largely a masculine occupation. Hypatia is the first woman mathematician of whom we have reasonably detailed knowledge, although not the very first of whom we are aware. We have, for example, sketchy information on the life of an earlier figure, Pandrosion, whose story is told in appendix B.

It is also regrettable that most of the lives of Hypatia that are reasonably available are based on unreliable sources. The best known such source is perhaps the book *Hypatia* by the Victorian novelist Charles Kingsley. This is a work of fiction, although its author of course undertook historical research in the course of its preparation.

But there is a tendency for fiction to pass into collective consciousness and to be transmitted as "legend," when there is no evidence for it. All too often legend then solidifies into reported fact. (For one of the more curious twists an earlier legend may have taken, see appendix C.)

Similarly, there are several supposed portraits of Hypatia, all of them drawn from artistic imagination. One has been given a wide currency, and indeed it is a work of great skill and charm, but it neither makes nor has any claim to authenticity.

My own research as presented here is based on the published versions of the primary sources and on reliable secondary sources. See the annotated bibliography and also appendix D, which gives the primary sources in English translation.

The sources tell us, or allow us to deduce, that Hypatia lived in the late fourth and early fifth centuries of our era. She was raised in the city of Alexandria, the daughter of an eminent mathematician. In due course she herself became a mathematician and (like her father) an astronomer as well. She wrote at least two books on mathematics and one on astronomy and she gave public lectures in philosophy. She had a large following and was a popular teacher, much admired by her students.

Although at this time Alexandria was part of the (Eastern) Roman Empire, its intellectual tradition was Greek, and Hypatia was very much a Hellene, both in her language and in her cultural heritage.

Her philosophy was Neoplatonic and her lifestyle dedicatedly celibate. She identified herself as a scholar and was accepted as such.

The political turbulence besetting Alexandria at this time ultimately claimed her life in the year 415 or 416 CE, when she was brutally murdered by a mob of Christian fanatics.

This briefly is the record of Hypatia. The chapters that follow will tell her story more fully, more analytically, and more critically, but first we should look at the background to that story: the times she lived in, the culture she inherited, and the events that preceded and followed her life. We need to look first at a broader canvas, and then, having appreciated where it is that our attention is to be focused, to examine the details.

*Chapter 1*

# THE HISTORICAL CONTEXT

*I*n the fifth century BCE, Greece was a collection of city-states of which Athens was the one we know best. It was in Athens that Socrates the philosopher lived and taught up till the time of his execution in 399 BCE. It was here, too, that his pupil Plato founded his Academy, an institution of higher learning with mathematics (in particular arithmetic and geometry) at the core of its curriculum.

Here also Plato's pupil Aristotle studied. Plato died in 348 or 347 BCE and Aristotle lived from 384 to 322 BCE. He in his turn taught Alexander of Macedon (Alexander the Great) whose dates are 356 to 323 BCE.

It was Alexander who united the various feuding states into a single Greek nation, which became the center of a large empire extending far beyond Greece itself.

In particular, Alexander's armies conquered northern Egypt around 330 BCE and one of his generals, Ptolemy I Soter, founded the city of Alexandria in the west of the Nile delta. Alexander installed Ptolemy as the first of a long line of hereditary rulers of Egypt. From that time till its takeover by the Arabs in 642 CE, Alexandria remained a Greek city and a major center of Greek learning and culture (often rivaling or even surpassing Athens itself). From its inception, however, its population included Jews, and Alexander himself decreed that Jews and Greeks were to be treated equally.

Early in his reign, Ptolemy I founded an institution of advanced scholarship, the Museum, which maintained a standard of excellence for almost seven centuries. It has been estimated that at the height of its glory the Museum in its libraries held some half a million books. The Museum, or at least its mathematical and philosophical traditions, will be dealt with in the next chapter.

Ptolemy also introduced the cult of a new god, Serapis, whose temple was adjacent to the Museum and whose worship was essentially peculiar to Alexandria.

The translation of the Hebrew scriptures (the Septuagint) in Alexandria in the third and second centuries BCE made these writings available to the Hellenic population as well as to those Jews who knew no Hebrew. A Platonistic account of Jewish religion (according to which the *Logos* or Word, the Idea of Ideas, was God's first-begotten) was produced in Alexandria by Philo Judaeus in the early part of the first century CE. Both these developments prepared the ground for the later spread of Christianity. Christianity came early to Alexandria. Tradition names Saint Mark the Evangelist as the first missionary to preach the Gospel there; more solidly, an early Alexandrian convert, one Apollos, is mentioned in Acts 18:24, as an assistant to the apostle Paul.

A little before this, in 80 BCE, Egypt was formally annexed to the Roman Empire as the Greek star by then had waned. Cleopatra's suicide in 30 BCE brought the Ptolemaic line to an end and Alexandria came under the direct governance of Rome.

However, this did not in any way affect the essentially Hellenic nature of Alexandria. It remained a Greek city with Greek as its language and with an intellectual tradition that was uncompromisingly Greek.

The first departure from this state of affairs came with the spread of Christianity. In the first century CE, Christianity was an insignificant movement, and it was only in the second century that it became deserving of notice. By the fourth century CE, however, it had become a very powerful force indeed.

The emperor Constantine I (Constantine the Great) embraced Christianity and "recognized" it—making it in effect the established state religion, a status it achieved de jure under the later emperor Theodosius I (Theodosius the Great). He also founded a city on his accession to the throne in 324 CE. This he erected on the site of the former Byzantium and modestly named it Constantinople. The new city became the focus of his power, and formed, along with Athens and Alexandria, the third major center in the eastern part of the Roman Empire.

Christianity remained the dominant religion of the empire thereafter except for brief lapses, notably a period during the reign of Julianus II (Julian the Apostate), 361–363 CE.

By this time the Roman Empire was in deep trouble. It was under external pressure from the Huns and the Visigoths and was in turmoil internally as well. In 364 CE it split into two parts: the Western Empire (ruled from Rome) and the Eastern Empire (ruled from Constantinople). Alexandria became a part of the Eastern Empire.

By this time, moreover, Christianity had developed an ugly face: the formerly persecuted were all too ready to become the persecutors. Jews felt the wrath of a by now openly anti-Semitic church militant, and "pagans," those who were neither Christian nor Jew, were also likely to be targets of violence.

As if this threefold division were not enough, points of doctrine divided the Christians and were all too often settled by force. Chapter 3, section A, gives more details of this, but these divisions between "orthodox Christians" and "heretics" further aggravated the factionalism that beset Alexandria in particular.

It was during the third and fourth centuries CE that the Museum fell into decline. The great libraries were destroyed in part during a succession of civil wars in the third century. The last collection probably went late in the next, in 391 CE, when the archbishop, Theophilus, obtained imperial sanction to raze the temple of Serapis and build a Christian church on its site (dedicated to John the Baptist, of whom he had custody of some alleged relics).

The last attested member of the Museum was a mathematician and astronomer, Theon of Alexandria, of whom we shall have much more to say, as he was Hypatia's father.

Early in the fifth century CE, in 412, Theophilus was succeeded in the archbishopric by his nephew Cyril (Saint Cyril of Alexandria).

Cyril was much at loggerheads with the civil governor (or prefect), Orestes. Orestes was a Christian, but a much more tolerant one than was Cyril, who seems to have been personally a most intemperate man.

In, possibly, 414, Cyril unilaterally took it upon himself to expel the Jews from Alexandria, and this he did, much to Orestes' displeasure. The ensuing riots and the feud between the two men were the direct cause of Hypatia's death and will be examined in detail in chapter 7, but the turbulence of the times owed as much to the rift between the secular and the ecclesiastical authorities as to the sectarian animosities of the people.

With Hypatia's death, Alexandria lost its secular intellectual tradition almost entirely. What little mathematical activity remained in the empire tended to be conducted elsewhere.

The relevant emperor at the time (see table 1) was the Eastern emperor Theodosius II, who had acceded to the throne as a small boy. His regent, Anthemius, ruled till 414 CE and probably continued to exercise de facto power after that, as Theodosius was then still only in his midteens. Anthemius's grandson of the same name became the Western emperor in 467 CE and reigned until his execution in 472 on the orders of the Suebian general Ricimer. These events may have a bearing on the Hypatia story.

Other later developments also germane to the matter are various letters sent by both Orestes and Cyril to Theodosius after Hypatia's death. These will be discussed in detail, along with the material of the previous paragraph, in chapter 7. Among Theodosius's attempts to quell the turbulence was an edict of 423 CE forbidding persecution of the Jews and destruction of synagogues—issued not so much out of compassion for the Jews as to quell riots and disorder among "Hellenes, Jews, and heretics." all of which groups he despised!

The Arabs captured Alexandria in 642 CE and much of what remains of the mathematics of the late Hellenic world has in fact reached us via Arabic translation. The intellectual tradition that characterized Alexandrian life for some seven centuries developed out of this historical content.

## COMBINED EMPIRE

| | |
|---|---|
| 324 | CONSTANTINUS I (the Great) |
| 337 | CONSTANTINUS II, CONSTANS I, and CONSTANTIUS II |
| 340 | CONSTANTIUS II and CONSTANS I |
| 350 | CONSTANTIUS II |
| 361 | JULIANUS II (the Apostate) |
| 363 | JOVIANUS |

| **WEST** | | **EAST** | |
|---|---|---|---|
| 364 | VALENTIANUS I | 364 | VALENS |
| 367 | VALENTIANUS I and GRATIANUS | 378 | THEODOSIUS I |
| | | 395 | ARCADIUS |
| 375 | GRATIANUS and VALENTIANUS II | 408 | THEODOSIUS II |
| | | 450 | MARCIANUS |
| 383 | VALENTIANUS II | 457 | LEO I |
| 394 | THEODOSIUS I (the Great) | | |
| 395 | HONORIUS | | |
| 421 | CONSTANTIUS III | | |
| 423 | VALENTIANUS III | | |
| 455 | MAXIMUS and AVITUS | | |
| 456 | AVITUS | | |
| 457 | MAJORIANUS | | |
| 461 | SEVERUS II | | |
| 467 | ANTHEMIUS | | |

**Table 1:** Roman Emperors of the Period

*Chapter 2*

# THE INTELLECTUAL
# BACKGROUND

*P*tolemy I Soter, in establishing Alexandria, gathered around him a group of learned men attracted from various parts of Greece. He inaugurated the great library of books mentioned in the previous chapter and erected the "Museum." This was a building in which the academics, for such they were, lived, studied, taught, and wrote. It was much more akin to today's universities than to the institutions that we nowadays call museums.

Later additions greatly expanded the holdings of the library. Aristotle's entire personal collection was acquired, as were the original editions of dramatic works previously held in Greek archives. A tradition developed compelling visitors to Alexandria to copy (by hand of course!) any books they might have with them, and to deposit the copies in the library.

Under the Ptolemies, the intellectual character of Alexandria was a literary and scientific one. Later, speculative and religious philosophies were cultivated. Throughout both periods, mathematics was very much a part of the intellectual life of the Museum and of Alexandria.

The first "professor" of mathematics was probably Euclid, who wrote a number of works, of which the best known are the *Elements*, the *Data*, and the *Optics*. The *Elements*, his most important and influential work, is a compilation in thirteen books of geometrical knowledge, the term "geometrical" here including considerable amounts of arithmetic. This has been one of the world's most celebrated works and even today there are school syllabuses based on it.

Not only did Euclid's *Elements* encompass a great scope of material, including as it did both two-dimensional and three-dimensional geometry, but it established a style of rigor and of presentation that is now seen as central to the mathematical endeavor. The entire edifice is constructed on the basis of a small number of axioms and postulates, mostly of an intuitively very plausible character; the extent of what is known is then systematically enlarged by logical derivation from these axioms and their consequences.

Other great mathematicians were also associated with Alexandria. The very greatest of all ancient mathematicians, Archimedes (287?–212 BCE), almost certainly paid a visit. Archimedes advanced mathematics in many directions and wrote many books in the area. His *On the Measurement of the Circle* (or *Dimension of the Circle*) may have some bearing on the story of Hypatia and will be mentioned again in chapter 9, section I.

Another early geometer was Apollonius of Perga, who was active around 200 BCE. Whereas Euclid's *Elements* had considered only straight lines and circles (what could be drawn with ruler and compass), Apollonius studied more complex curves, known as conic sections because they may be generated by slicing through a cone. Apollonius's work has a direct bearing on Hypatia's story and will be dealt with in more detail in chapter 9, section D, and appendix A, section B.

An approximate contemporary of Apollonius was Eratosthenes, who was both a mathematician and a geographer. He is remembered for the "sieve of Eratosthenes" (a method for constructing the sequence of prime numbers: 2, 3, 5, 7, 11, 13, 17, 19, 23, 29, etc.) and as the first person accurately to measure the size of the earth.

Another geographer was also the greatest of ancient astronomers, Ptolemy (or Claudius Ptolemaeus), who lived from about 100 CE to about 170 CE. He also worked in Alexandria and is the Ptolemy after whom the Ptolemaic system of the universe is named. We, living five hundred years after Copernicus began its overthrow, have little time for the older picture which placed the earth at the center of the universe, with the sun, moon, and planets moving round it in more or less complicated "epicyclic" paths.

However, this is more than a trifle unfair. Much practical astronomy remains geocentric to this day and, furthermore, it would in fact be quite possible to make small adjustments to the Ptolemaic theory to make it observationally indistinguishable from the Copernican. Our grounds for preferring the latter come in large part from the relative simplicity of the heliocentric description and from the impact that the new viewpoint had on the development of physics.

Ptolemy wrote a number of works, notably the *Syntaxis* (which we know better by its Arabic name, the *Almagest*) and the so-called *Handy Tables*. We shall see these again in chapter 9, sections B, C, E, and appendix A, section A. He also wrote an astrological work, the *Tetrabiblos*, which is pertinent to chapter 6; he was as well the author of one or more works on the astrolabe (an astronomical instrument) and these will also be discussed in more detail, in chapter 9, section G, and appendix A, section D.

Diophantus of Alexandria, who flourished around 250 CE, wrote an *Arithmetic* that is seen as significant in several ways. One is that it takes the first steps toward algebraic notation and symbolism by abbreviating what would otherwise be long and clumsy verbal descriptions. Another is that it set up equations to be solved under conventions different from those that had hitherto been employed. This work is most relevant to Hypatia's story and it also will be further discussed, in chapter 9, section F, and appendix A, section C.

After Diophantus we have Pappus, a mathematician of the early fourth century CE. He observed an eclipse that has been accurately dated to 320 CE, but other information on when exactly he lived is rather confusing and contradictory. His most important work is known as the *Collection* and it is precisely that: a concatenation of eight otherwise unconnected books that are often our only source of knowledge about the mathematical research of his own and slightly earlier times. It seems to have been designed more or less as a companion volume— something to aid the study of original works to which the reader was assumed to have access (but which are lost to us).

Other works by Pappus are of the type we know as "commentaries." These, too, are derivative works, intended to assist the student in mastering some particular earlier work. A "commentary" is somewhat akin to an "edition," but differs in that the primary purpose of an "edition" is to present the original text (which had of course to be copied by hand). An "edition" however could and often did incorporate explanatory notes, or *scholia*, to assist the reader. In the case of a "commentary," the scholia became more important and it was not always the case that the original text was presented in its entirety.

In practice, the line between the two genres could become somewhat blurred, and, furthermore, different "commentators" or "editors" (or the scribes who copied their work) took greater or lesser care to differentiate the scholia from the original text. In many instances, nonetheless, commentaries are important as a source of knowledge of the original, and in a number of cases are the only source of that knowledge. Pappus wrote commentaries on Ptolemy's *Almagest*, Euclid's *Elements*, and Euclid's *Data*.

The rise of the commentary as a genre signals a considerable change of emphasis; whereas, say, Diophantus's *Arithmetic* is a product of research and Euclid's *Elements* a work of synthesis and logical reorganization, a commentary is exactly what its name implies. Essentially it is a textbook, deriving from an earlier classic and designed to assist the student to read and understand the original work; in some cases, such works are very like lecture notes and quite possibly this is exactly how many began their lives. The proliferation of commentaries shows a shift of emphasis away from primary research and into the giving of priority to the conservation and transmission of knowledge. This change of intellectual emphasis occurred as the city of Alexandria was becoming more turbulent and its Museum became threatened with destruction. (For more on Pappus, see chapter 5 and appendix B).

Theon of Alexandria worked in the late fourth century CE; the question of giving more precise dates will be discussed in chapter 5. He was prolific both as an editor and as an author of commentaries. Until the early nineteenth century his edition of Euclid's *Elements* was our only access to the original text. He also produced editions of two of Euclid's other works, the *Data* and the *Optics*, as well as commentaries on each of Ptolemy's *Almagest* and *Handy Tables*. There are also other works now lost or partly so; particularly relevant to our purpose here is a work, or perhaps two works, on the astrolabe, which we will encounter again both in chapter 9 and in appendix A. Yet more works have been assigned to him but the attribution is doubtful.

Theon of Alexandria is usually seen as a minor mathematician, important only because his editions and commentaries had great influence and provide us with information about more important original works by others. This is more fully discussed in chapter 10.

Theon's successor as principal mathematician in the city was his daughter Hypatia, who was not associated with the Museum (whereas her father and Pappus before him had been). She taught and lectured in what is usually called the Neoplatonic School, but it is quite possible she conducted her classes from her home. Her death saw the end of significant mathematical thought in Alexandria; the later mathematicians Proclus and Eutocius practiced elsewhere, Proclus leaving Alexandria for Athens. Eutocius however may have studied in Alexandria; we will encounter him again in chapter 9, section D.

The teaching of Neoplatonic philosophy in Alexandria began with the philosopher Ammonius Saccas, whose death is placed as occurring probably after 242 CE. Since we have no writing from his hand, we can know only indirectly of his thought through the influence he exerted on his pupil Plotinus. It is known, however, that he abandoned Christianity in favor of his Neoplatonic views, which were therefore of a religious nature.

Plotinus's philosophy was also of a religious nature; his system is briefly sketched in the next chapter. He left Alexandria for Rome in 243 CE. Hypatia is placed by some authors in the Plotinian tradition, but others have seen the Alexandrian philosophical school as reverting to an exegesis of the works of Plato and Aristotle. There are widely disparate views as to the philosophical system Hypatia herself espoused, and this matter is looked into in chapter 8.

Hypatia's successors in the Alexandrian philosophical tradition were Olympiodorus the Elder and Hierocles of Alexandria; the latter's Neoplatonism is seen by some as having been influenced by Christianity. (Mathematics was taught by an otherwise unknown Heron; he was not the well-known figure of the same name.) But about the time of Hypatia's death the center of Neoplatonic thought moved to Athens, where the best remembered of the scholarchs were successively Proclus, Marinus, Isidorus, and Damascius. In 529 CE, the emperor Justinian, enforcing Christianity as the state religion, closed the Athenian Neoplatonic School and Damascius went temporarily into exile in Persia. We shall meet him again in chapter 4.

Even though the Museum was effectively dead from 391 CE onward, we still find Synesius of Cyrene, after this date, comparing the intellectual climate of Athens very unfavorably with that of Alexandria. Synesius was Hypatia's pupil, the best known of her many, and he almost palpably worshiped her, so that perhaps his is a colored view, but it does accord with the fact that Hypatia was clearly more eminent both in mathematics and in philosophy than any of her contemporaries.

Later, however, Plutarch of Athens greatly revivified the Athenian Academy, and Proclus, finding little stimulus in the lectures of Olympiodorus or of Heron in Alexandria, left that city to study in Athens. Although Neoplatonist philosophy did later revive in Alexandria, this was somewhat later than the period under consideration.

Religion formed an important component of the intellectual endeavor at the time when Hypatia lived. Let us now look at this.

# Chapter 3
# THE RELIGIOUS BACKGROUND

## A. CHRISTIANITY

*T*he principal belief separating Christianity from the other two great monotheistic religions, Judaism and Islam, is the doctrine that Jesus of Nazareth was in fact the incarnation or embodiment of God. The question of what precisely this meant (and how it could be) was one the Christian church faced in its early centuries when it set about developing a consistent formulation of its central tenets and embarking on a systematic theology. Eventually orthodox belief on the question was encapsulated as two dogmas: the doctrine of the Trinity and the doctrine of the Hypostatic Union.

The doctrine of the Trinity is normally expressed by saying that God comprises three distinct persons sharing a single divine nature; the doctrine of the Hypostatic Union, by contrast, sees Jesus as a single person endowed with two natures, the one human and the other divine. These formulaic statements will mean little to those who have not studied or shared in the tradition that enshrines them, so further explanation is in order.

The early Christian church wished to make the claim that Jesus indeed *was* God, yet it was at the same time committed to strict

31

monotheism and had no desire to be seen as worshiping two gods—the one of the Hebrew scriptures and the other the person of Jesus.

The doctrine of the Trinity is the firm assertion of monotheism in the face of this dilemma. Essentially, and in nontechnical language, it maintains that there is a single God who is knowable (insofar as our finite intellects can be said to "know" God) in three distinct ways. These ways correspond to three separate eras in human history—for, even more than Islam, Christianity has human history at its very center.

First, there is God as known in the pre-Christian era: the God that can be apprehended through the exercise of human reason or via the revelations made to the Hebrew prophets and other such recipients of divine grace. This is the God of the Old Testament.

Second, there is God as manifest in the life of Jesus, as seen by the apostles and other disciples, who evidenced divine power by a healing ministry, by inspired preaching, and, most centrally, by rising from the dead. This is the God of the Gospels.

The third route to God is the witness of believing Christians, an apostolic tradition derived unbrokenly from those who saw Jesus in the flesh, and manifest in the power of their belief to radically transform their lives. This is the God of the other books of the New Testament.

These three aspects of God are referred to by Christians as, respectively, God the Father, God the Son, and God the Holy Spirit (or, less aptly, Ghost). The reasons for these names need not detain us here, but the key to the understanding of the doctrine is that all are perceived as aspects of the one indivisible God, who is the same God worshiped by both Jews and Muslims. Christians would of course claim that, being in possession of all three routes to the deity, they have the advantage over these other groups, who have but one.

Section C will return briefly to the doctrine of the Trinity.

Turning now to the doctrine of the Hypostatic Union, and again simply accepting terminology to avoid long digressions, the point at issue is to assert the one-ness of Jesus' person, but simultaneously to assert both his divinity and his humanity. He is not to be thought of as a sort of divine Jekyll burdened with a human Hyde. Nor is he God walking the earth simply disguised as a man. Nor is he a man merely favored (like, say, Muhammad) by God. Orthodoxy insists that he be viewed in each of two lights: as fully human, and also as fully divine.

The discussion and argument that led to these formulations occupied much of the fourth century CE and continued into the fifth. Cyril of Alexandria is very much a key figure in the delineation of orthodox doctrine; this is the reason for the exalted place he holds in the calendar of Christian saints. He supported these orthodox views not only by reasoning and debate but also by means of a military and full-frontal "muscular Christianity."

Those who adopted unorthodox views, the heretics, were engaged in battle, both verbal and physical. During his life, Cyril waged mighty wars against three groups of heretics: the Arians, the Novatians, and the Nestorians. Shortly after his death, his diocese fell into the hands of a fourth such group, the Monophysites. (He may well not have had so many differences with this last group. They are alive and well today as the Coptic Church. The Copts claim Cyril as one of their greatest saints and doctors; indeed, they took custody of relics from his body, and these are still greatly venerated among them today.)

Each of the heretical groups just mentioned (except for the Novatians, who will be discussed later) opposed in one way or another the dogmas of the incarnation as outlined above.

The Arians solved the problem of Jesus' theological status by "dividing the substance"—that is to say, the "nature" in the terminology used before. They denied that, in the words of the Nicene Creed (a litany of central orthodox beliefs), Jesus was "consubstantial with the Father," and for them he was not fully God. Rather, he was more like a Roman demigod, or perhaps a sort of "projection" or shadow of God. Therefore, they denied both the Trinity and the Hypostatic Union.

The Nestorian heresy, like the Arian, involved a denial of the dogma of the Hypostatic Union. Nestorians held that Christ was really two persons, one human and one divine, who happened to share the same body.

The Monophysites also denied the Hypostatic Union but had yet another solution to the problem of Jesus' nature. For them (as their name implies), he had but one nature rather than two. He was neither human nor divine, but a unique hybrid of the two.

Finally the postponed Novatians. This group did not fall out with orthodoxy over major dogma, but rather over an issue of church policy. When they were ultimately denounced as heretics, the point of departure was much less fundamental. What the fuss was about was the status of those Christians who had defected in times of persecution and who, now that the going was good, wanted back in. The Novatians would have no truck with these fair-weather sailors, and one tends to sympathize.

Theologically the issue became one concerning forgiveness of sin. Ultimately, orthodox opinion, as represented by Cyril and others, upheld the right of the church and its appointed officers to exercise the divine and apostolic power to forgive sinners.

The contention between orthodoxy and the various heresies was conducted with a violence and a bitterness that will hardly be apparent in the above bare outlines of doctrinal divergence. Why, we might ask, get so "het up" about details of a "hypostatic union" that few people understood anyway?

The question is a valid one, but ultimately is beside the point. The differences between Protestant and Catholic in today's Belfast have but trivial relation to doctrinal distinctions between these rival sects. So it was in Alexandria. What the various groups were really at loggerheads over was the question of who owned the churches and who controlled what went on inside them. In other words, matters of real estate and policy. But there is also the point that one could hardly expect Arians to participate in a liturgy that included the recitation of the Nicene Creed.

Arianism was widespread for much of the fourth century CE. However, the council of Constantinople in 381 reaffirmed the Nicene

Creed. Shortly afterward, Arianism fell under an imperial edict and its star began to wane. Even so, Cyril continued to write anti-Arian polemics until 428.

Cyril's moves against the Novatians were among the first initiatives undertaken upon his accession to the archbishopric in 412, when he closed the Novatian churches and seized their sacred vessels (which may easily have represented considerable wealth). This was an even earlier exercise of power than his expulsion of the Jews.

His conflict with the Nestorians occupied much of the later years of his reign and stimulated much of his theological thinking and writing. In 431, deputizing for the pope, who was absent, he chaired the council of Ephesus that condemned the Nestorians. This movement, like the others, waned, although small numbers of Nestorians remain to the present day.

Cyril died in 444 and has long been accorded the title of saint. This was given him long before Rome adopted its present formal canonization procedures. But he stands in good odor still with the Roman church. In 1882, Pope Leo XIII formally pronounced him a Doctor of the Universal Church, and in 1944 he was the subject of Pius XII's encyclical *Orientalis ecclesiae* issued to commemorate the fifteen hundredth anniversary of his death.

Although a good deal of his writing (of which there is much: a bilingual Latin-Greek anthology of his surviving work occupies almost all of ten large volumes) is polemical, Cyril's theological expositions, biblical exegeses, and spiritual essays are regarded as more significant. They are the basis of the respect in which he is held today.

The question of his complicity in Hypatia's murder will be explored in chapter 7.

# B. NEOPLATONISM

Plato's philosophy is built upon the activity of *abstraction*—our ability to form an *idea* of something. The wider the notion we form, the closer we come to the essence of its being. It is this *idea* that is the key element; it transcends the instances on which it is based.

The notion can perhaps best be illustrated by reference to mathematics. Abstracting from our encounters with pairs of objects, we learn in early childhood to form the concept of the number 2. As we grow older, probably as we learn elementary arithmetic, the number 2 becomes quite real to us. We "reify" it and come to talk about numbers like 2 and 3 as actual entities, even though we never encounter them as such; we encounter only pairs of objects together exhibiting a property of "two-ness," and so on.

Although there are many possible accounts of the nature of mathematics, it is this Platonist view of the subject that most practicing mathematicians embrace as a working philosophy. It informs the very language of mathematical discourse: we speak of "the properties of the circle" as if the circle was a thing, something quite familiar, to which it is quite natural to attribute properties, or we might refer to "the discovery of Pythagoras's theorem," as if prior to this Pythagoras's theorem had been, so to say, sitting out there like America waiting to be discovered.

This mathematical example is by no means the only one that could be given. We similarly form ideas of "truth" or of "beauty" and speak of these as actually existing. ("Can you put a price on beauty?") But the mathematical example is probably the clearest case and certainly it is the most fully developed. This is the reason for the centrality of mathematics in Plato's scheme of education.

Thus, Plato's world is a world of ideas, and he accounts the material world of our senses as merely a projection or shadow of that world. We come to know the world of ideas by abstracting from that shadow. If we then abstract once again from the world of ideas, we form the idea of ideas. This for Plato is Being-in-Itself: the One. It is ineffable and transcendent, and it is identified with the Good.

The account just given argues *to* the One *via* the process of abstraction (the formation of ideas), which is indeed our human approach, but actually it is, so to speak, to look through the wrong end of the telescope. It is truer to say that the One exists and that the ideas emanate from the One. These ideas find instantiation in the material world.

Platonism, so described, clearly has a religious element to it. (It posits a central ineffable One that is also identified with the Good.) And if one seeks to know and to find union with the One, then the activity of thought and of abstraction takes on a holy significance. This is true of mathematics, perhaps especially true of mathematics, because it is the most powerful and elaborated example of the process of abstraction and of transcendence above the material world. Mathematics, thus seen, becomes a profoundly sacred pursuit.

Platonic doctrine was elaborated in many different directions. The term "Neoplatonism" is now used specifically to refer to the developments initiated by Ammonius Saccas in the third century CE and found in the writings of his pupil Plotinus and others in that same tradition. As the term is used, it also refers to avowedly religious interpretations of Platonist philosophy. (Although almost certainly the system taught by Ammonius had precursors, and quite certainly there were religious elements in Platonism from its very inception.)

For Plotinus there was a central deity: Absolute Unity or Unity-in-Itself. From this emanates Intelligence, which is the *Logos* (or Word), which reveals the One (i.e., the Unity). Goodness is the One, but "the Good" is to be identified with Intelligence. Ideas are contained in Intelligence.

From Intelligence in its turn emanates the Soul—the *Logos* of Intelligence. Individual souls are contained in the Soul. The Unity, the Intelligence, and the Soul coexist eternally, and the priority given above is logical rather than temporal. Together they form the Trinity.

Of its very nature the Soul is creative and so the world emanates from it of necessity. All creatures tend to return to the Unity, although the human soul by the intervention of evil was forced away and needs to return, something that can be achieved either in this life or following reincarnation. It is the nature of our souls to seek the intelligible and the divine.

Plotinus's theory of matter differed from Plato's. Whereas Plato had studied nature for its own sake, Plotinus's philosophy was essentially panpsychic, with matter not being real. Reality comprised ideas.

Plotinus's views were expounded, and in the process altered, both by his successor Porphyry and by the later Iamblichus, and other figures as well. Neoplatonism as a movement never sought the doctrinal uniformity that Christianity held so crucial, and thus it is not clear from a description of someone who was a Neoplatonist quite what that individual's beliefs may have been. This is particularly the case with Hypatia of whose beliefs we have no direct record. This will be discussed more fully in chapter 8.

Neoplatonist beliefs could be held alongside an adherence to the Greco-Roman pantheon of gods, or else independently of this. Some Neoplatonism was quite syncretic and incorporated elements of Chaldean lore, Zoroastrianism, Egyptian religion, and even Indian features, together with various Hellenic inputs. Other versions, by contrast, abandoned the pantheon to concentrate on purely mystical elements. Such doctrines taught that the soul could, by making itself responsive, return the more speedily and readily to the One, which could be known only via a mystic union with it.

Where Neoplatonism abandoned the aspects of pagan worship, it was much less objectionable to Christians, who were prohibited from using the theurgical practices some Neoplatonists employed. But when these were divorced from the intellectual content, Christians could find in the latter much that they could accept and use in the formulation of their own doctrines. Section C of this chapter gives a brief account of one such influence, and there will be further discussion in chapter 9.

Although Porphyry wrote anti-Christian polemics, there were nonetheless Christians who were quite happy to take elements of his teaching and to adapt it for their own purposes. One of these was Hypatia's pupil Synesius, who will be discussed in section C.

Iamblichus's doctrine is less well preserved than Porphyry's, but he gave an exalted place to mathematics in his cosmogony. For him, numbers were generated by the One, via a principle of plurality. Geometric objects were similarly generated by, for example, unit points. Thus, the One generates the truth of mathematics and the beauty of geometric form and so the study of mathematics becomes a path to true virtue (although there were other paths, such as the Greek gods and the Egyptian mysteries).

The ability to pick and choose among the elements of Neoplatonic thought means that the same term covers a wide range of individual philosophies. Central to this were the notions of the One (which could easily be identified with the God of monotheistic tradition) and the concepts of emanation and creativity. These, too, could easily be reconciled with Christian doctrine and put to work in Christian theology, and very often they were. We turn now to a brief discussion of one such case.

# C. THE DOCTRINE OF THE TRINITY

The account of the Trinity given in section A of this chapter does scant justice to the enormous literature and vast history that lies behind Trinitarian doctrine. To attempt a review here would be to take the discussion far from its main purpose, but it is in order to remark that the simplified summary given above bears only small resemblance to the doctrine as usually expounded. It meets the twin aims of making the doctrine accessible to outsiders (who all too often see it as some kind of mathematical conundrum, which of course it is not) and of making sense of many of the biblical texts that are held to bear upon the matter.

However, the usual accounts discuss the Trinity in quite different terms. The versions one finds most readily are already much more highly elaborated and present the doctrine as a type of revelation of God's inner structure, supplying further detail of the divine nature. One such account goes like this.

God, who is all knowing, is seen as, in particular, knowing himself, and this knowledge is understood to be of so perfect a character that it constitutes a replica, so to speak, of the God who is doing the knowing. It is not, however, a second God, but, again in the words of the Nicene Creed, "consubstantial." The two persons, for this is the term by which they are designated, then have such a perfect love for one another that this love constitutes a third "person," coequal with the other two.

Again, the relations described are logical, rather than temporal, and indeed are said to be imposed upon us merely by dint of the finitude of the human mind. The three persons are, respectively, God the Father (the One), God the Son (the Knowledge, *Logos* or Word), and God the Holy Spirit (the Love). This formulation, which has clear Neoplatonic affinities, is usually expressed by saying that the Son proceeds from the Father and the Spirit from the Father and the Son equally and jointly.

It has a long and complicated history, but this form of the doctrine, which one finds in liturgy as well as in exegesis, is recognizable in the thought of Augustine (Saint Augustine of Hippo), an exact contemporary of Hypatia. Its roots, however, are visible as early as the Gospel of John.

Hypatia's pupil Synesius had a somewhat different formulation—one that derives directly from Porphyry. Porphyry, like Plotinus, had a triad or Trinity as part of his system. His differed in detail, however. (Such details still in fact divide some of the Eastern from the Western branches of Christianity.) Synesius taught that from the One (Being, also referred to as the Father) emanated Power (identified with Life—the *idea* of life, of course, not the multiplicity of living things) and from Life emanated Intellect (or Thought).

Synesius, in his account of the Trinity, identified God the Father with the One, God the Son with Power, and the Holy Spirit with Thought in this Porphyrian scheme. Augustine was also influenced by Porphyry, but his account differs from that of Synesius, being essentially the one sketched above.

We might say that Synesius's account is linear, while Augustine's is triangular. It is the Augustinian version rather than the Synesian that comes closer to the expositions used today. In particular, the triangle is a common iconographical symbol for the Christian God.

These are but two of many schemata that have been proposed; almost all of the various accounts, however, contain strong Neoplatonist elements. Synesius's version, though not now invoked in the West, was one input, and an important one, into the modern formulation of the doctrine. In fact, enunciations akin to it still find a place in some of the Eastern churches.

Now that the historical background has been filled in, it is time to narrow the focus and concentrate more particularly on our subject.

# Chapter 4

# THE SOURCES

*W*e have so far placed Hypatia in Alexandria during a particularly turbulent period at the end of the fourth and the beginning of the fifth centuries CE. She was a pagan, a Neoplatonist philosopher in a city where Christians both orthodox and heretical, secular and ecclesiastical authorities, pagans of highly diverse views, and Jews all coexisted in mutual enmity. She had inherited a great and ancient intellectual tradition, though it was sadly depleted, and she continued to teach and write in a climate of increasing difficulty. Her syllabus embraced mathematics and astronomy as well as the formal study of philosophy—a philosophy with strong religious overtones.

In this chapter, we look in more detail at how we know these things about Hypatia, what else we can say, and how much detail we can give to elaborate this bare outline. We begin with the primary sources, which can be divided into two categories: writings by Hypatia and writings about her.

In respect to the former, we are poorly served. What seems to be part of one of her works has come down to us, and there are more or less doubtful attributions of other material. All of this is technical stuff—its subject matter mathematics or astronomy. The most likely example of her writing is in fact the part of Theon's Commentary on Ptolemy's *Almagest*, which covers Book III of that work.

The *Almagest* comprises thirteen books in all. Inscriptions at the start of Theon's commentaries on Books I–II directly ascribe the subsequent material to Theon himself. Books IV–XIII contain no inscriptions whatsoever of this type. Book III is omitted in most manuscripts, but one, on which today's edited text relies, includes it and it bears an inscription by Theon saying that the work is his own but in, or with, the edition of "my philosopher-daughter Hypatia."

The details of this work and of other works sometimes attributed to Hypatia will be covered in chapter 9 and appendix A. As Book III of Theon's Commentary on the *Almagest* is a technical work of astronomy (concerned with the motion of the sun) it is relevant to an appraisal of Hypatia's mathematical standing and to other aspects of her thought and technical accomplishment. It tells us very little of her life. For that, we must turn to the other category: the primary sources that tell us *about* Hypatia.

These may be grouped under two headings. On the one side is the *Suda Lexicon*, on the other the (better-preserved) writings of the early Christian church. (The relevant passages are all given in English translation in appendix D.)

The *Suda* is a tenth-century encyclopedia arranged alphabetically and compiled from various sources. It was formerly referred to as the *Suidae Lexicon* and attributed to an eponymous Suidas. (Much as if some thirtieth-century historian were to speak of Britannicus and his wonderful encyclopedia!) Modern research, however, relates the name "Suda" to the Greek word *souda* for "fortress": a "Stronghold of Knowledge," so to speak. However, many authors, including many contemporary authors, retain the earlier name. The definitive variorum edition gives the various readings of the original derived from different available manuscripts, and also follows this convention in the name.

The *Suda* entry on Hypatia is a long one, deriving from at least two independent sources (as the layout adopted in appendix D emphasizes). It has been the subject of considerable critical scrutiny and there is no unanimous agreement as to detail.

The broad outlines, however, are clear. The first and shorter of the two sections into which the entry naturally falls derives mainly from an earlier (sixth-century) encyclopedia, the *Onomatologus* of Hesychius of Milesius. Hesychius of Milesius is also known as Hesychius the Illustrious, but must be distinguished from Hesychius of Alexandria (who, confusingly, has nothing to do with the story) and other such namesakes. His *Onomatologus* has not survived in its entirety, and modern reconstructions use, for example, the *Suda* to make good deficits in what survives of the original. Hesychius is usually seen as a pagan author.

The second and longer of the two sections is believed to derive principally from a largely lost work: a *Life* of the philosopher Isidorus by his pupil Damascius (both of whom we met briefly in chapter 2). This is unambiguously a pagan source, for Damascius suffered exile at the hands of the Christian emperor. Damascius's *Life* has been the subject of various attempts at reconstruction, based on quotations in other works, such as the *Suda*, as well as on a summary referred to as the *Abridgment* of Photius. (Photius was a ninth-century Christian scribe.) The extract from the *Life* that found its way into the *Suda* entry contains most but not all of the extant material now ascribed (with varying degrees of certainty) to the original. It also includes, however, as its final two paragraphs material that is not really germane (see appendix D, section A).

The Christian histories are much better preserved than the pagan (for obvious reasons) and all but one of the relevant passages are to be found in the compendium *Patrologiae Graecae* (or PG for short). This is a collection, running to over 150 volumes, of Greek writings important in the history of the Christian church.

The most direct and complete account of Hypatia in the PG is that of the ecclesiastical historian Socrates Scholasticus (not, of course, the Athenian philosopher who drank the hemlock some 840 years before his namesake picked up the pen). He gives a fuller account of Hypatia's death than does Damascius, and also provides a vivid and detailed description of the turbulence that preceded it.

His *Ecclesiastical History* is dated to about 440 CE, some twenty-five years after Hypatia's death, so it almost but not quite attains the status of a contemporary record. Slightly earlier, but very imperfectly preserved, is an account by another ecclesiastical historian, Philostorgius. What we have of his version of events reaches us as a summary written by Photius.

A brief sentence by the sixth-century historian John Malalas tells of Hypatia's death. It is clearly independent of the other sources, but it may also be less accurate, as it is incompatible with more circumstantial accounts in aspects of detail. Other brief mentions occur in the works of tenth-century Theophanes and fourteenth-century Nicephorus Gregoras. The (in this context very late) sentences by Gregoras can hardly qualify as primary sources and are essentially passing references.

One Christian history of the period that gives a detailed account of Hypatia's death is not included in the PG. It is preserved in Ethiopic translation and not in Greek, and it was also the product of a bishop of the Coptic Church and thus was regarded as a heretical document (see chapter 3). This is the narrative of seventh-century John of Nikiu. We saw in the previous chapter that the Copts inherited the mantle of the Monophysite heretics and continue even to this day to venerate Cyril of Alexandria. John of Nikiu's account is thus not surprisingly highly favorable to Cyril. It derives principally and quite directly from Socrates' *History*, but adds material disparaging Hypatia—material to be considered in detail in chapter 6.

This version of events is in fact unique in its attitude to Hypatia. Of the Christian sources it is the least known and the least influential. All the others tell of the life, and death at Christian hands, of a prominent advocate of a rival philosophy. Moreover, they do so in such a way as to leave a favorable impression of her: the impression that informed, say, Kingsley's novel or the passage in Gibbon's *Decline and Fall*.

The other primary source, on a word count the longest, in the PG consists of various writings by Hypatia's pupil Synesius. Six of his letters (and a fragment of a seventh) addressed to her are extant and she is also referred to in four letters directed to other correspondents. We learn from this material that he sent her copies of a work *On Dreams*, an essay-letter *De Dono Astrolabii* (concerning, of course, an astrolabe, and also mentioning Hypatia), and sought her opinion of his work *Dion*, a philosophical tract.

I do not include in my list of primary sources either two brief mentions by Nicephorus Gregoras (dismissed above) or four other works which are also sometimes listed as such.

Cassiodorus, a sixth-century historian, gives an account (available both in the PG and in its companion, the *Patrologiae Latinae*) that is simply a Latin translation of Socrates' Greek. (It is sometimes listed separately because Cassiodorus incorporated it in a larger work.) The fourteenth-century writer Nicephorus Callistus merely paraphrases and embroiders upon the same source.

I also discount, as does every other historian on the subject, an alleged letter from Hypatia to Cyril dealing with the Nestorian heresy. Not only was it written after her death but also its contents are quite incompatible with what we know of her life.

Nor do I regard the epigram of which a translation appears following the title page of this book as a true primary source, although it may testify to the regard in which Hypatia came to be held (it is not entirely certain that it is addressed to the same Hypatia as the heroine of this book).

Otherwise, the primary sources about Hypatia are those documents discussed above and to be found in English translation in appendix D. Of course, we need not believe everything they say simply because they are primary sources. For a start, there are matters on which they contradict one another. On one point, for example, the second part of the *Suda* entry is directly at loggerheads with the first. Moreover, historians, then as today, record opinion in the same breath as fact. They select what facts they deem relevant to their purpose, and indeed present their judgments under the guise of fact. Doubtless when John of Nikiu wrote: "[Hypatia] beguiled many people through her Satanic wiles," he saw himself as reporting fact; we, however, may demur.

There is an obvious lacuna in all the primary narratives: after

Hypatia's death, what happened next? None of them say. They see her martyred and, that done, they go on to other, quite different matters. Here we need to rely on more indirect evidence. This was compiled by the sixteenth-century ecclesiastical historian Baronius (Caesar Cardinal Baronius) from imperfectly preserved and very different primary data. This work will be considered in detail in chapter 7.

For other secondary sources, see the notes and the annotated bibliography.

We are now in a position to move on to the main part of the story: the details of Hypatia's life and death, and to assess her achievements.

## Chapter 5

# THE DETAILS OF HYPATIA'S LIFE

The most detailed accounts we have of Hypatia's life are the records of her death. We learn more about her death from the primary sources than we do about any other aspect of her life. Socrates in particular goes to considerable pains to date it: "This happened in the month of March during Lent, in the fourth year of Cyril's episcopate, under the tenth consulate of Honorius, and the sixth of Theodosius."

Honorius ascended the Western throne in 395 (see chapter 1, table 1) and Theodosius II became Eastern emperor in 408. From lists of the consuls appointed at this time it has usually been deduced that March 415 is the most likely date to agree with the numbers given by Socrates. However, Cyril became archbishop in October 412 and so was in the fourth year of his episcopate in March 416. This date has from time to time been suggested, perhaps even more authoritatively, but today 415 is almost universally accepted as the date of Hypatia's death. The usual opinion is that in saying "fourth" when he really should have said "third," Socrates made a rather easy-to-fall-into arithmetic error. We, in our way of giving dates, may easily make the same error: 12, 13, 14, 15—four years, count them! Thus consensus has it that she died in the year 415.

That she was the daughter of Theon of Alexandria has never been disputed. Hesychius states it explicitly, as do Socrates, Theophanes, and Philostorgius; Damascius offers a partial confirmation. Theon himself proudly acknowledged the relationship in the inscription to Book III of his Commentary on Ptolemy's *Almagest*: he speaks of the contribution of "the philosopher, my daughter Hypatia."

Two dates in Theon's life are known with great accuracy, although unfortunately they occur within months of each other. In his *Small Commentary* (he wrote another *Large Commentary* as well) on Ptolemy's *Handy Tables*, he records seeing two eclipses, one of the sun and one of the moon. These have been very precisely dated. The former occurred on June 16, 364, and the latter on the night of November 25–26, 364. Thus Theon was actively practicing astronomy in the year 364. In a similar way it may be established that the earlier mathematician Pappus was active in 320.

The *Suda* entry on Theon is somewhat garbled, but it makes him a contemporary of Pappus and credits both with achievements in the reign of Theodosius I (378–395). Now Pappus can hardly have been born much later than 295, and even granting him a long life (which he may well have enjoyed—"Pappus" means "grandfather") he would surely have been most active much before 378, although he and Theon could have been contemporaries in the sense of being colleagues, the one some forty years or so older than the other.

There is another passage in Theon's *Small Commentary* that relates to an "astronomical conjunction." This, too, has been accurately dated, in this case to 377, a date consistent with Theon's having been active during the reign of Theodosius I (see chapter 1, table 1). However, there is some doubt as to the authenticity of this passage; if it is spurious, one might be inclined to place Theon's active period earlier, closer to the one year of which we are certain.

Against this it may be urged that Theon was a prolific author and that this betokens a long productive life. He produced at least eight editions of or commentaries on the works of Euclid and of Ptolemy and possibly published other books as well. Moreover, his commentary on the *Almagest* ran into at least two editions, the second incorporating the material produced by his daughter.

Of Hypatia herself, the *Suda* says she flourished in the time of the emperor Arcadius (usually listed as 395–408, but Arcadius was actually proclaimed emperor in 383, during his father's lifetime).

There are different possible resolutions to the various constraints imposed by these pieces of data: both the certain and the less certain. Hypatia's birth has been placed as early as 350 and as late as 375. Most authors settle for "around 370." This scenario would be consistent with Theon's having been born around 340, observing the eclipses as a relatively young man, seeing the birth of his daughter when he was about thirty, and living to collaborate with her in about the early 390s when she was in her early twenties and he in his early fifties. This dating would have him about forty years old on the accession of Theodosius I and about fifty-five when Theodosius died and Arcadius succeeded to the throne (if indeed he lived that long—we have little idea when Theon died).

Alternatively, if Hypatia were born about 350, we would have to push Theon's birth back to about 325. This would make him about forty years old when he observed the eclipses and a little over fifty when he saw the conjunction (if indeed he did). He could still have been active in the reign of Theodosius I and would have been sixty-five or so when the temple of Serapis (and effectively the Museum) was destroyed.

Hypatia would in this scheme of things have been about forty when the Museum was closed forever and could well have been collaborating with her father on astronomical work for up to twenty years. If Theon's death coincided approximately with the final destruction of the Museum, she would have come into her own and have been perceived as an independent thinker at about the time of Theodosius's death and Arcadius's accession.

Both the *Suda* and Socrates paint a picture of an attractive and already independent woman, and this has been interpreted as making her young at the time of her death. This is not incompatible with the picture they (particularly Socrates) give of a woman of great political influence. All this favors the 370 date of birth.

Against this, however, are other lines of evidence—and the "young at death" image need not carry quite the weight that at first sight it might appear to do; one need not be young to be beautiful. But the brief sentence by John Malalas describes Hypatia as an "old woman" at the time of her murder. One must of course be careful not to read too much into this: Malalas says Hypatia was burned alive and this statement is at variance with the careful, detailed, circumstantial, and convincing description given by Socrates. Nor is it clear what in the context is meant by "old."

Yet if we adjoin a further line of evidence, then the balance tips, to my mind, in favor of a date before 370, even if not quite as early as 350. This concerns her pupil Synesius. Synesius's many letters are full of references to contemporary events. He was made a bishop in (probably) 411 or 412, when he would have had to be older than thirty, the minimum age under canon law. Using such considerations, careful study of Synesius's writings has given a reasonably definite chronology, which has him being born around 370 and studying under Hypatia probably in the early 390s. His letters to her span the years 399 to 413 and indeed she was the recipient of his final letter, penned from his deathbed.

The letters addressed to her seem very much the writings of a younger man to an older teacher. Though they often ask for greetings to be conveyed to various friends, they never mention Theon. One presumes that Theon was already dead. (Thus, if Theon lived a long life, we need to push back the date of *his* birth and so also his daughter's.) This conclusion is reinforced by the strong feeling throughout the letters that for Synesius, higher learning in Alexandria *was* Hypatia. We find no reference to any other teacher.

Thus, on balance, I prefer the view that Hypatia was born significantly before 370, perhaps as early as 350.

Of Hypatia's mother we know absolutely nothing. Speculation that she assisted Theon in her daughter's education is precisely that: speculation. Similarly with the hypothesis that in fact she died in childbirth. There is no evidence for any such assertions and, where made, they are pure fiction.

There is, however, some slight evidence that Theon had a son, and thus Hypatia a brother, named Epiphanius. The introduction to Theon's commentary on the *Almagest* dedicates the work to "Epiphanius, my dear son" (a dedication repeated at the start of Book VII of that work). Another similar dedication appears in his *Small Commentary* on the *Handy Tables*.

At first sight this would seem to be conclusive, but in fact this is not so. The Greek word here translated as "son" is *teknon*. This term, while it could refer to biological sonship, was also used as an affectionate form of address from a senior to a junior man (much as the word "son" may be so used in vernacular spoken English today). Thus Epiphanius may simply have been a favorite pupil.

When Theon spoke of Hypatia (in the inscription to Book III of his commentary on the *Almagest*), the word he used was *thugater*, which means unambiguously "daughter" in the full biological sense. The corresponding word for "son" would be *pais*, although even this word could be used in a complimentary rather than a literal sense.

Thus we can't really know if the Epiphanius of the dedication was Hypatia's brother or not; perhaps the probabilities, on balance, are a little against it.

Nor do we know much about Epiphanius. Although the name was a relatively common one, none of the obvious candidates fit the facts. From the dedications themselves we deduce an interest in astronomy. Damascius gives a brief account of an Epiphanius who was involved in the Egyptian cult of Osiris. This may or may not be the same person, and may or may not be the same person as a shadowy figure who wrote a treatise on "thunder and lightning." This is really all we can say on the matter. There is no trace of a brother in the accounts we have of Hypatia's life; nor does a brother (an astronomically adept brother) complicate either the close professional relationship between father and daughter or the teacher-pupil relationship between Hypatia and Synesius.

Hypatia's education in mathematics came from her father. Damascius attests to this, as does Philostorgius. In fact, this would almost

have to have been the case, for after Pappus's death Theon was unrivaled as the leading mathematician of his time. He held this position
indeed until the mantle passed to Hypatia herself.

The *Suda* entry on Theon describes him as a "philosopher," a word
which has two related but distinct meanings: on the one hand, it may
be understood in the technical sense of current usage, and on the other,
it has the generic meaning of "thinker." When Theon is described as a
"philosopher," it is surely in this second sense. He emerges as a specialist mathematician and astronomer, the author of commentaries—
essentially student guides to mathematical classics.

When we come to Hypatia, however, we are on different ground.
Damascius writes: "In nature more noble than her father, she was not
satisfied with her education in mathematics by her father but also
gained a knowledge of philosophy, the other not ignoble study." True,
Damascius does take some of this back later: "Isidorus greatly outshone Hypatia, not just as a man does over a woman, but in the way a
genuine philosopher will over a mere geometer."

Women and mathematicians alike will delight in a nineteenth-century gloss to this infamous sentence: "It means in plain language that
Isidorus knew nothing of mathematics."

However, it is most evident that Hypatia's interests did extend
beyond mathematics (although her best work undoubtedly lay in that
field). It is quite clear that they embraced Neoplatonic philosophy,
though whether her Neoplatonic education was derived from other
teachers or through her own reading we simply do not know. Socrates
places her in the tradition of Plato and Plotinus and goes on: "She
explained the principles of philosophy to her auditors, many of whom
came from a distance to hear her instructions." Damascius also has her
"expounding in public to those willing to listen on Plato or Aristotle or
some other philosopher."

One of those "willing to listen," who indeed "came from a distance to hear her instructions," was Synesius of Cyrene, her best-
known pupil, and an eminent Neoplatonist philosopher himself (even
after his conversion to Christianity). His letters to her clearly presup-

pose a shared Neoplatonism and they make it manifest that he learned his philosophy from his "mother, sister, teacher and withal benefactress," namely, Hypatia.

She was perceived as a beautiful woman: "exceedingly beautiful and fair of form" (Damascius). Socrates puts it a little differently: "[She had] self-possession of manner, which she had acquired in consequence of the cultivation of her mind . . . [she was admired] on account of her extraordinary dignity and virtue." As we shall see, this was her persona in a life lived very much in the public eye.

Almost certainly Hypatia never married; in fact, as shown in the next chapter, she was dedicatedly celibate. This does, however, mean that Hesychius is wrong in one detail, for he makes her Isidorus's wife. She certainly can't have been the wife of the Isidorus whose *Life* Damascius wrote, for this Isidorus was some thirty-five years unborn when Hypatia died. Nor is there any other plausible Isidorus who might be adduced to fill the role. This statement moreover is quite at odds with the other sources. Damascius tells us: "though naturally modest and fair minded, she remained unwed."

It was once the rule to attempt to reconcile these two contradictory statements in a variety of ingenious if implausible ways. It is more usual today for scholars simply to discount Hesychius's rogue phrase.

Aspects of Hypatia's lifestyle and public appearances will be dealt with in chapter 6; the events culminating in her death will occupy chapter 7.

# Chapter 6
# HYPATIA'S WORK, ATTITUDES, AND LIFESTYLE

The Hypatia we first encounter in the primary sources is already mature, learned, and independent. She is an acknowledged expert in mathematics, astronomy, and other (nonmathematical) branches of philosophy. John of Nikiu, whose account will be considered later in this chapter, disapproved greatly of Hypatia; yet even he nowhere questions her competence. The other historians speak of her with clear admiration and without for one moment questioning her skill or her authority.

They remark on her womanhood and rightly so, for it was unusual for a woman to hold such a profession, but they do so without condescension. True, at one point, Damascius refers to her womanhood as a natural disadvantage not shared by his idol Isidorus, but there is none of Dr. Johnson's "It is not done well; but you are surprised to find it done at all." She is variously described as a philosopher (Hesychius, Damascius, Theophanes, Synesius, and Malalas), a teacher of philosophy (Synesius), a mathematician and astronomer (Philostorgius), an astronomer (Hesychius), a learned woman (Socrates), and a geometer (Damascius). Even John of Nikiu refers to her as a female philosopher.

Hypatia is not the only woman "philosopher" of antiquity. Theanno was an associate (possibly the wife) of the early mathematician Pythagoras; Pandrosion has been briefly mentioned and is the subject of appendix B; Hipparchia (wife of a philosopher named Crates) is reasonably well known; one Eudocia Palaeogina (daughter of Neocaesarita Prosecretarius and wife of Constantius Palaeologus) is introduced by Nicephorus Gregoras as "another Theanno or another Hypatia"; and Proclus was taught, following his move to Athens, by a woman called Asclepigenia; and indeed there are other examples.

Very little is known of most of these women. But it is very clear that Hypatia at least, if not these others, asserted her right to teach publicly and that this assertion was not questioned. "Donning the *tribon* [the robe of a scholar, and thus an essentially masculine item of apparel], the lady made appearances around the center of the city, expounding in public to those willing to listen on Plato or Aristotle or some other philosopher." "There was a great crush around the doors [of her house], 'a confusion of men and horses,' of people coming and going, and others standing about . . . [for] Hypatia the philosopher was now going to address them, and . . . this was her house." In these terms Damascius describes her obviously popular public teaching.

These lectures would naturally have been on philosophy; one hardly imagines such vast crushes of people jostling to hear her address them on mathematics or even astronomy. Her public profile and the visible character of her teaching brought her honor and influence in Alexandria, enhanced by her own dignity of deportment. Damascius describes her: "In speech articulate and logical, in her actions prudent and public-spirited, and the rest of the city gave her suitable welcome and accorded her special respect. The archons handling the affairs of the city would always go to see her first . . . for if the practice of philosophy had declined, still its reputation was seen to be revered and respected by those managing the important affairs of the state."

Socrates concurs: "She not infrequently appeared in public in the presence of the magistrates. Neither did she feel abashed in coming to an assembly of men. For all men on account of her extraordinary dignity and virtue admired her the more. . . . She had frequent interviews with Orestes [the prefect]."

Nevertheless, her principal scholarly activity lay not so much in her public lectures or in any civic activity but in specialist areas of mathematics. Hesychius mentions three works from her pen: a commentary on Diophantus, another on "the astronomical table" (possibly this is the interpretation), and a commentary on Apollonius's *Conics*.

The astronomical work may or may not have been the revised version of her father's commentary on Ptolemy. This will be discussed at length in chapter 9. The other two are works of pure mathematics, and for their day advanced mathematics at that. These also will be considered in detail later in this chapter. There is *some* rather slender evidence for other technical writings on mathematics, but none at all for any work on philosophy. She taught the subject and her lectures were well received, but we have no hint at all that she ever wrote on it.

There may well have been philosophical comment in the letters she sent to Synesius; indeed, it would be strange if there were not, but these would be private, or at best semipublic, documents, and in any case they have neither survived nor ever been listed as publications. His letters to Hypatia do deal with philosophical topics, but also with scientific ones. While he sent her a copy of his philosophical tract *Dion*, he also discussed scientific instruments, specifically an astrolabe and a "hydroscope." These letters will be addressed in detail in chapter 9, sections G and H, and appendix A, section D. He also sent her a copy of his essay *On Dreams*, a would-be scientific work that will be discussed later in this chapter.

There were four branches of mathematics in antiquity: arithmetic, geometry, astronomy, and music. The three works attributed to Hypatia by Hesychius cover one-for-one the first three of these. (For Hypatia's possible involvement with music see below.) Of these four branches, we may see the first two as being "pure mathematics" and the others, astronomy in particular, as being "applied." The "pure" branches proceed by the process of abstraction from real instances as outlined in chapter 3, section B. The objects of their study are already Platonic ideals: numbers, lines, geometric figures, and the like. The rationale for their study is seen not only in curiosity for its own sake, but rather as a sacred pursuit leading the soul to the One—curiosity as the manifestation of the soul's innate yearning for intelligibility, which is the route to the divine.

The subject matter of astronomy is, if readers will pardon the oxymoron, more mundane. Its objects of study are material structures: the sun, moon, stars, and planets. Moreover, it is an essentially *practical* study; it is undertaken not only for its own sake but also with a view to constructing clocks and calendars and aiding navigation, among other things. Not that arithmetic and geometry are impractical. Rather, arithmetic in the hands of Diophantus and geometry with Euclid and his successors have already transcended and surpassed the humdrum considerations of accountants and land surveyors.

Astronomy did not then attain this level of abstraction and indeed never has; it retains its material referents. It did, however, have, like arithmetic and geometry, spiritual significance. According to Synesius: "Astronomy itself is a venerable science, and might become a stepping stone to something more august, a science which I think is a convenient passage to mystical theology, for the happy body of heaven has matter underneath it, and its motion has seemed to the leaders in philosophy to be an imitation of mind. It proceeds to its demonstrations in no uncertain way, for it uses as its servants geometry and arithmetic, which it would not be improper to call a fixed standard of truth." Thus one could ascribe a spiritual dimension to astronomy, but it also retained its practical utility. Astronomy is to be seen as a *science* and we may in large measure characterize the goal of science, then as now, as the quest *to know the future.*

We can know the present by direct experience and contemporary report; the past through memory and the historical record. The greater challenge is to find out beforehand what is going to happen. The science of astronomy was the first to achieve clear success in these terms.

Seen from earth (and in those days before electrical lighting and smog one saw much more clearly from earth), the stars form a fixed pattern in the sky. This pattern may be observed to move as a whole but the structure of the pattern itself remains constant. Against this backdrop, the moon may be observed to travel through various of the constellations or "houses"—that is, distinct sections of the overall pattern. Similarly, if one pays closer attention, one will notice five exceptional, or wandering, stars (the planets Mercury, Venus, Mars, Jupiter, and Saturn) that also move about over this fixed background. The sun, of course, is not present in the night sky, but the points of its rising and setting may also be seen to alter with respect to the pattern of the stars. These seven heavenly bodies were collectively known as "the planets" (Greek *planetes*, "wanderers").

The study of the paths described by the sun and, to a lesser extent, the moon is vital for the construction of accurate calendars. These in their turn are a sine qua non for the organization of any complex society. In particular, in Egypt, the whole of the region's agriculture depended on the accurate prediction of the annual Nile flood.

By the time Ptolemy had completed his work, not only were the motions of the sun and moon utterly predictable, but they were predictable with such accuracy that eclipses (formerly strange and frightening aberrations) had become explicable and could be foretold. In addition to this, planetary positions could be calculated in advance.

This was clearly a major advance (albeit in a limited area) and it is a natural impulse to press so promising a research program further. That the sun and moon influenced human affairs was obvious and so it was quite reasonable to assume that the five planets did likewise.

Today we find uses for data on planetary positions—establishing accurate chronologies by references to "conjunctions," determining exact longitudes by the observation of a "transit of Venus," or the like. But all this lay centuries in the future. What was advanced at the time to fill the void was astrology.

It can hardly be emphasized too much how pervasive was the influence of astrology in the ancient world and how widespread the credence it commanded. In particular, Ptolemy wrote a work, the *Tetrabiblos*, devoted to the subject. Astrology was seen as providing useful predictions, especially in the human sphere, even if these were less precise than those of astronomy. The Christian position was one of opposition to the practice of astrology (although not all Christians complied). Much of the justification for Hypatia's murder as advanced by John of Nikiu carries the imputation that she practiced astrology. He also charged her with devotion to "instruments of music," and so raises the question of Hypatia's involvement with the fourth and last of the branches of mathematics. Damascius, too, mentions music in his account of Hypatia, but essentially to discount it, and in a somewhat different context.

Hypatia was, as we have seen, unmarried, but was at the same time "exceedingly beautiful and fair of form." This combination was, as we may well suppose, a source of temptation to some of the young men with whom she mixed. And so we learn that "one of her colleagues [or perhaps students] fell in love with her. And he could not control his passion, but made his affections obvious to her. Some uninformed stories say that Hypatia cured him of his sickness with music, but the truth long ago reported that tales of music were nonsense, and that bringing out one of her menstrual napkins she threw [or thrust] it at him; and having displayed the evidence of her unclean nature said: 'It is this you love, young man, not beauty'; and he, put off by shame and horror at this unseemly display, disposed his heart more temperately."

The incident has embarrassed a number of Hypatia's more adulatory biographers. It sits oddly, for example, with Gibbon's "modest maid." In fact, from 1753 until very recently, no author in English recounted the story without either being extremely vague over detail or else lapsing into patristic Greek at some point, thus seeking to hide potentially prurient or libidinous material under the dead language of scholarship.

Nevertheless, we should try to find the import of this story. It may well disquiet some of today's feminists (and others) that a woman should find her vagina (even her menstruating vagina) "unclean" and "not [of] beauty," but we need to observe the case without using twenty-first-century eyes.

Other cultures preserve the evidence of a girl's first period and even ascribe special power to this relic. An Athenian cult of the goddess Artemis (the equivalent of the Roman Diana) attributed special healing properties to a woman's so preserved first menses. Possibly Hypatia's action fell within some such tradition.

However, we may plausibly take speculation further. Until quite recently, menarche occurred much later in a girl's life than is the rule in Western societies today. Sexual maturity was achieved only as a girl approached marriageable age. Furthermore, there was no really effective contraception, and so, since both pregnancy and lactation inhibit ovulation, menstruation was actually a relatively rare event.

A woman who menstruated regularly would thus (infertility aside) be a celibate woman and her monthly periods the insignia of a forsworn lifestyle (certainly in Hypatia's case, as she obviously didn't want for suitors). Such a choice has long been the hallmark of the Roman Church, which has institutionalized it with its insistence on a celibate clergy and celibate orders of other religious groups (monks, nuns, lay brothers, and certain lesser orders below the rank of priesthood). This state of affairs is currently under some challenge, but there is still a point to the traditional argument that celibacy allows a concentration of effort on the spiritual and intellectual demands of the religious life.

The Christian church, however, can claim no monopoly on this way of thinking and it makes perfect sense for a Neoplatonist, committed to a transcending of the material world, to embrace a lifestyle that minimized her involvement with it.

This account of the matter makes the menstrual napkin a powerful symbol, but not an instrument of magic. Damascius dismisses the rumor of music, which John of Nikiu sees as another, different instrument of (satanic) magic. But we do need to look in more detail at the implied question: the charge of astrology is one that has been raised and not only by John of Nikiu. Furthermore, this author justifies, indeed triumphs in, a deed that most others have found hideous and shameful—Hypatia's murder. In doing so he calls upon a tradition that held mathematics to be evil, and certainly Hypatia was a mathematician.

Midway through the fourth century the council of Laodicea outlawed divination, the attempt to use thaumaturgical means to the end of knowing the future. The thirty-sixth canon of that council forbade priests to be mathematicians. One of Hypatia's contemporaries, Augustine (Saint Augustine of Hippo), tried a neat bit of casuistry before disillusionment set in: "Those impostors whom they call 'Mathematicians' I consulted without scruple: because they seemed to use no sacrifice nor to pray to any spirit for their divinations: which art, however, christian piety consistently rejects and condemns."

Clearly these mathematicians were doing something other than studying Euclid's *Elements* or Ptolemy's *Almagest*. The leading mathematicians of the era (Pappus, Theon, and Hypatia) certainly pursued mathematics in its scholarly and reputable aspect. Did they also dabble in the other side and practice astrology?

There is some very shaky evidence to connect Theon to astrology. The *Suda* reports that he wrote a work titled *On the Signs and Observation of Birds and the Call of Crows*. This may or may not have been a work of divination; we don't know, as the work is lost. Nor is it clear that it is properly attributed to Theon of Alexandria and not to some other Theon. But Theon's major work falls into a very clear and recognizable pattern: he was out to preserve and to adapt for student use the great classics of Alexandrian mathematics—Euclid and Ptolemy. The endeavor is entirely reminiscent of today's "Great Books" programs.

As we shall see, Hypatia continued this work with the later and more demanding classics by Apollonius and Diophantus. However, neither father nor daughter ever sought to produce a commentary on the *Tetrabiblos*. I attach great weight to this piece of negative evidence.

We may also consider in this context Synesius's theory of dreams. It was expressed in a work written (so he claimed) at a sitting in a surge of inspiration and sent immediately to Hypatia for her approval, which, it would seem, was received. Synesius definitely saw it as a scientific theory, even a mechanistic one. Its physiology is of course outdated (along with other aspects), but that is irrelevant to the point to be made here.

Synesius saw spirit (*pneuma*) as emanating from the blood of all animal organisms and conferring life upon them. *Pneuma* was a material substratum and it was here that sensory and intellectual activity met. It formed a sixth, inner, sense, as distinct from the five external senses (sight, sound, touch, taste, and smell) and it acted to join sensory and intellectual data into an intelligible whole. Its "language" comprised phantasms or inner images, which are the means by which we attain understanding. These phantasms house the interactions between the upper world of the universe and the lower world of humankind, and thus it is through these phantasms, which we access in dreams, that we experience the interaction of the two worlds.

This theory then makes the dream a scientific instrument, that is, one by which the future may be known. Dreams for Synesius form the natural means of divination, open to all; a dream "demands no long journeying abroad, to the oracle of Delphi or the shrine of Ammon; all I have to do is to wash clean my hands, to pray aright, and then to fall asleep."

The knowledge so gained was not as precise as, say, that used to predict eclipses, but dreams (rather than astrology) became the key to learning what lay ahead in human affairs—a natural, accessible, and universal means, beyond even the power of the emperor to interdict.

We do not now accept this theory and may find it quaintly dated, but before we let our twentieth-first-century smugness run away with us, we should recall that Freud's theory of dreams has commanded a great and recent following, and it may well be questioned whether it is any better.

In any case, if Hypatia acquiesced in Synesius's theory of dreams, then she can hardly have been a serious astrologer.

The picture that we form of Theon and Hypatia is one of a team working against the odds to preserve valid mathematics in a climate where the genuine article was becoming a rarity and pseudomathematics was flourishing in its place. These distinctions, obvious enough to us, would not have been at all clear to those too ignorant to appreciate the difference: a category that includes John of Nikiu and very likely the murderers whose actions he extols.

Hypatia's case then was this. She lived in a time when her intellectual heritage, a seven-hundred-year-old tradition, was crumbling. The supports that had once seemed so secure—the Museum and the libraries—had all been swept away by the swell of ignorant dogmatism. Almost alone, virtually the last academic, she stood for the intellectual values, for rigorous mathematics, ascetic Neoplatonism, the crucial role of the mind, and the voice of temperance and moderation in civic life. By competence and by force of personality, she could command a crowd; her popular lectures and charismatic presence drew the multitudes. She held the ear of the legitimate authority and was heard with respect.

But that tide of opinion which knows no possibility of doubt, which adheres blindly and mindlessly to a cause, which abandons intellectual quest for the assurance of a mute and unquestioning "faith"—all this was against her; and her life became forfeit to the bloodlust of those who would claim, with the ironic certainty of unconscious self-refutation, their access to a higher morality.

# Chapter 7
# HYPATIA'S DEATH

*I*n considering the political turmoil of fifth-century Alexandria—
the conflicts between Christian and pagan, between Christian and Jew,
between orthodox and heretical views, between the ecclesiastical and
the civil authorities—in getting an understanding of the various factions and of the bitternesses that inflamed each group, a modern parallel may be illuminating.

The situation in Malaysia today presents a number of striking
resemblances. Before I develop it, however, let me hasten to add that
in several important areas, the analogy breaks down.

First and most crucially, today's Malaysia does not resort to violence in the resolution of its conflicts. Alexandria was quite otherwise.
Second, the city's religious factions were not anything other than that;
they did not (except for the native Egyptians, who hardly enter the
story, and possibly for the Jews) correspond to ethnic groups, whereas
in Malaysia they do. The Christians of Alexandria, the pagans too, the
secular and the religious authorities, the orthodox and the various
groups of heretics: all these were Greeks. Third, unlike Malaysia,
Alexandria owed allegiance to distant Constantinople; Malaysia, of
course, is an independent and sovereign nation.

Otherwise, the analogy is remarkably close. Malaysia has in effect
an established religion (Islam) and there is continual debate as to
which matters are the proper province of the secular authorities and
which of the separately constituted Islamic institutions. This is similar

to the situation in Alexandria, except that the religion in question there was Christianity.

Then, too, Islam has great concern for purity of doctrine although it contains sects that mainstream believers dismiss as heretical. The denunciation of error is one of the important roles undertaken by religious leaders. Again, the parallel is close.

There are in Malaysia enough Buddhists to compose a large minority group, often resentful of the power of Islam and of the privileged status it enjoys. Their own often more flexible and less dogmatic religion is, to their eyes, more open to intellectual endeavor and less concerned with doctrinal conformity and overelaborate niceties of formulation. They are thus the counterparts of the pagans of antiquity.

Next, a smaller group of Hindus occupy the position of a third component of the population. Their status is not unlike that of Alexandria's Jews. The current geographical and historical enmity between Hindu and Muslim may be taken as a parallel to the hatred of Christians for Jews, and vice versa.

Finally, the indigenous Egyptians may be thought of as the counterparts of the *orang asli*, or native Malaysians, who are a politically insignificant group in most of peninsular Malaysia, just as the native Egyptians are almost (and somewhat puzzlingly) entirely absent from our story.

The civil governor, or prefect, of Alexandria at the relevant time was Orestes. He was a Christian, but as has already been mentioned in the previous chapter, took frequent counsel with Hypatia, who was not. He showed concern for all his subjects, including, as we shall see, the Jews. His Christianity was of a tolerant variety that did not seek to proselytize. His methods seem to have been essentially those of compromise.

Orestes was, however, a man of his time and, like any governor of the period, did not hesitate to resort to torture or to execution if he deemed it merited and necessary. This may shock us, but again we should not subject a fifth-century figure to twenty-first-century criteria. The Malaysian parallel holds good here, too; that country has no qualms over the use of flogging or of hanging where due process of its law demands it. This causes much disquiet among Western observers, yet few Malaysians (whatever their group affiliations within their own country) share this concern.

In 412, Cyril of Alexandria succeeded his uncle Theophilus as archbishop. Theophilus had already adopted a hostile and militant approach to the pagans. With imperial sanction, but at the cost of causing great disorder and concomitant loss of life, he had seized, lost, retaken, and finally demolished the temple of Serapis (in the process, in all probability finally putting an end to the Museum). In other words, he could command the resources to diminish rival religions by force. Most particularly, Theophilus armed a band of Nitrian monks and thus had at his disposal a powerful militia, owing allegiance to him rather than being under the control of the legitimate imperial authority.

It is clear that this situation continued into the episcopate of Cyril, one of whose first actions as bishop was to close the Novatian churches and to plunder them. The Novatians, of course, were unwilling victims of this exercise; the closing required coercive force and Cyril must have been in a position to exercise it.

We have no record of Orestes' response to this development, but it could well be that he may have viewed it as a matter internal to the Christian church, orthodoxy taking action against heresy, and so requiring no intervention on his part. Such, however, was not the case with Cyril's next action, which involved the Jews.

The level of community tension must have been extraordinarily high, for savage intercommunal violence erupted from an initially trivial episode.

The Jews, who conducted no business on their Sabbath, were in the habit of attending public dancing exhibitions on that day. Quite what the nature of these was we don't know, but they in some way or another scandalized certain of the Christians, who took it upon themselves to suggest that the Jews would be better employed in "hearing the Law." The dancers, however, were very popular and attracted great crowds on Saturdays—crowds that became rowdy. (Perhaps we find a parallel in the soccer hooliganism of today.)

Orestes, countering these complaints, imposed limitations upon the performances (but not to the point of putting a stop to them). These restrictions were resented by the Jews. The public proclamation of one such restriction upon the dancing shows attracted not only the regular patrons but also scouts from Cyril's party, anxious to learn the precise nature of the decree to be issued.

One of these scouts was a particularly officious and notorious individual named Hierax, whose presence among them angered the Jews in the audience. They raised the alarm that this man was there not to observe, but only to incite a riot.

If such indeed was his purpose, Hierax succeeded in accomplishing it, although not immediately, and certainly not in a way he would have intended. Orestes took a different view of Hierax's presence and saw him as a spy sent by Cyril to report on the initiatives being undertaken by the civil government, whose power the bishop was all too eager to usurp. He had Hierax arrested and publicly tortured—an action that greatly angered Cyril.

Cyril, possibly because it was the easier road, blamed the Jews for the misfortune that had befallen his lieutenant and took it upon himself to intimidate them, calling their community leaders before him and threatening them. This course of action backfired, however. Jewish extremists meeting in a secret conclave plotted and carried out a massacre of Christians.

The conspirators used palm-bark to fashion finger rings that were the sign by which they would recognize each other. They waited until after dark, and while the city slept raised an alarm that one of its principal churches was ablaze. As Christians emerged from their homes to help save the building, they were seized upon and slaughtered. Failure to wear the distinguishing palm-bark ring invited attack for anyone abroad that night.

It was Cyril, rather than Orestes, who was the quicker to respond to this atrocity. Accompanied by a large and angry crowd of Christians, he marched on the synagogues, seized them, and systematically expelled the Jews from Alexandria, further motivating his followers by encouraging them to loot Jewish homes and synagogues.

Orestes, caught off-guard, felt that Cyril had greatly overstepped the mark. The Jews, though a minority group, were a significant, indeed important, part of the city's population and a major loss to its economy. He no doubt would have liked to clip Cyril's wings, but it would seem that he had no immediate means to do this. He thus took the slower route of writing to Constantinople to enlist the help of the distant metropolitan power.

Cyril likewise wrote to the emperor, presenting his version of the incident and dwelling on the massacre perpetrated by the Jewish extremists.

The initiative back in Alexandria still lay with Cyril, who, from his position of strength, sought a reconciliation with Orestes. There is no record that he offered any concessions at all, and so powerful was his position that it is very likely that he offered none. In such a circumstance, any gesture by Orestes could be seen only as a token of surrender and this the governor naturally refused to give.

A second such initiative from Cyril upped the ante, for the bishop again sought a reconciliation with the prefect, this time extending to him the book of the Gospels, in which they both believed, as the basis on which their rift should be ended. Such an offer of reconciliation would have placed Orestes in some difficulties, for it should not be forgotten that the governor, as a Christian, owed his spiritual allegiance to the bishop and in matters of Christian morality and church discipline was obliged to take direction from his adversary.

Theoretically, when it came to matters temporal, the shoe was on the other foot. But for Cyril (and in theory at least for Orestes), spiritual matters were infinitely more important than temporal, so that the obligations of the latter could in good conscience be ignored. Moreover, the bishop held considerable power in the temporal sphere as well as in the spiritual, de facto if not de jure.

Orestes, however, again refused Cyril's offer, no doubt regarding it as the manipulative ploy that it was. Cyril's response was a further escalation of his forces. The Nitrian monks, who retained their arms from his uncle's day and who manifested "a very fiery disposition," were once more called upon, and some five hundred of them left their monasteries and made for Alexandria, thus greatly increasing the size and the strength of the forces that Cyril could mount.

These new arrivals quickly confronted Orestes himself. The action began with insults; either unaware or oblivious of Orestes' Christian affiliations, they taunted him with charges of paganism and idolatry, ignoring his protestations to the contrary. What was already an ugly melee turned into a full-scale assassination attempt a brief while later when Ammonius, one of the monks, hurled a stone, gashing the prefect's head and producing a copious flow of blood.

Things must have looked bad for Orestes at this juncture, for the majority of his guard took to their heels. It was the partisan crowd of bystanders who came to the prefect's rescue, not only saving his life and scattering the monks but also managing to apprehend Ammonius.

Orestes again asserted his authority by the public torture of one of Cyril's supporters. In Ammonius's case, the torture was so severe that the man died.

Cyril, upon learning of this, got hold of the body and placed it in a position of honor and veneration in one of his churches. He conducted over it a ceremony of canonization, bestowing on the would-be assassin the title of Saint Ammonius Thaumasius (Saint Ammonius the Admirable) and publicly declaring him to be a martyr for the Christian faith.

This was, of course, an exercise of Cyril's spiritual power, but it was a hasty and an ill-considered one. For there were at that very time Christians who pointed out that Ammonius was hardly a martyr within the meaning of the act: he had never been called upon to renounce his faith and thus could not possibly have died in consequence of a refusal to do so. Cyril did not rescind his action, though he quietly let the matter drop and "suffered the recollection of the circumstance to be gradually obliterated by silence."

Politically, Cyril, in his canonization of Ammonius, publicly implicated himself in the attack on Orestes, although in all probability he neither ordered it nor even knew about it until after the event. The rift between the two leaders deepened and widened, and in the process claimed Hypatia's life.

Though matters had looked bad for him earlier, Orestes ended up the clear winner in the dispute with Cyril. Those who had come to fight in Cyril's cause must have felt the bitter rancor of defeat. Another attack was called for and this time against a somewhat easier target.

That target became Hypatia. She was close to Orestes without *being* Orestes; she was genuinely a pagan and not a Christian merely labeled as pagan; she was less likely to be protected by armed men (for we may be sure that Orestes would by now have strengthened his bodyguard); her public appearances made her an easy mark; her devotion to mathematics was open to simplistic misrepresentation. She publicly expounded Neoplatonist philosophy (i.e., a set of teachings that rivaled those of Christianity) and indeed had influenced Christian thinkers, such as her earlier pupil Synesius—thinkers whose views were more tolerant and tentative than those of the invincibly self-righteous Cyril.

Orestes was probably no theologian, but he seems to have carried into the realm of public administration and civil life those principles of pluralism and tolerance that Cyril so obviously dismissed. In this Orestes was seen to be abetted by Hypatia, and the rumor spread that it was her influence that prevented the governor from reaching out and grasping the olive branch that Cyril had so publicly and so theatrically offered.

Thus it happened that a crowd of Christian zealots, led by one Peter the Lector, blocked the homeward path of the carriage in which Hypatia was riding, dragged her from it, and (as if to seek divine sanction for their act) hauled the hapless woman into a church where they stripped her naked and battered her to death with roofing tiles. This done, they continued their frenzy by tearing her corpse limb from limb, orgiastically transporting her body out through the church portals and burning its fragments.

The record about Hypatia's death becomes silent at this point. However, we do learn that Orestes again appealed to the emperor. Evidently he lacked the resources to challenge Cyril head-on. Nor, of course, could Hypatia be brought back. What he did seek was the administrative resource of obtaining some restraint on Cyril's dangerously powerful private militia—almost certainly the band of Nitrian monks.

It may be that the emperor's seeming inaction on the matter was, as was whispered, the result of his former regent, the still powerful Anthemius, having been bribed. It was later seen that the execution of Anthemius the younger, grandson of the earlier figure, was retribution for the death of Hypatia. (See the account in chapter 1.) This reconstruction need not compel our belief.

The imperfectly preserved public record indicates that in 416 Orestes had some partial success in limiting the number of members of, and in obtaining some measure of direct control over, a group known as the "parabolans." In 418, however, these decisions were overturned; the number of "parabolans" was allowed to increase and their control reverted to the archbishop. In 423, as already mentioned in chapter 1, the emperor was still trying to impose some sort of order on Alexandria: this time, by outlawing persecution of the Jews who by this date had returned.

The word "parabolan" means "one who exposes himself to danger" with the implication that this may be in pursuit of some higher cause. Its major application was to those who undertook the care of the sick and the dying and thus risked contracting infectious disease themselves. However, there is an ambiguity here. A "front-line soldier" may equally be seen as one who courts danger in service to some higher loyalty.

Orestes is hardly likely to have petitioned the emperor in order to reduce the number of selfless Florence Nightingales in his province. The second meaning is therefore much more plausible: that he sought imperial help in curbing the sway of a dangerous and hostile militia.

Cyril for his part could plead ignorance—these "parabolans" were nothing but a group of holy monks whose vocation it was to minister to the afflicted. (Indeed, this may well have been the case, when they were safely back in their monasteries in Nitria!)

But by far the most ink has been spent in debating back and forth the question of Cyril's personal guilt in Hypatia's slaying. For myself I despair that the truth will ever be known, but we will make some progress by distinguishing two quite different questions that most of the many discussions contrive to confuse.

Church authorities may seek to discover, though secular historians must not, how Cyril stands before the throne of God. The Church claims access to special means of knowledge in such matters, but these means lie outside the toolkit of those of us who merely read the record. Thus I prescind entirely from the pronouncements of the Vatican, the tradition of veneration and the alleged miracles brought about through Cyril's intercession, and treat the matter in a purely secular way.

Judgments on Cyril's complicity are almost universally made "along party lines." Those whose affiliations lead them to venerate his memory exonerate him; anticlericals and their ilk delight in condemning the man.

The closest to a balanced judgment that one finds in the literature would seem to be that of nineteenth-century Anglican historian Canon William Bright: "Cyril was no party to this hideous deed, but it was the work of men whose passions he had originally called out. Had there been no onslaught on the synagogues, there would doubtless have been no murder of Hypatia."

I would put the root of the trouble earlier than that. The attack on the synagogues was in fact provoked by an atrocity on the Jewish side. The extremists who initiated *that* were responding to the growing danger as Cyril expanded his temporal power in opposition to the legitimate secular authority, and made Jews the scapegoats when he disliked the actions of the prefect.

Cyril's place as a doctor of the universal church rests on his theological work. In doctrinal formulation he ranks with Augustine and Aquinas; his spiritual writings are accounted profound and wise; his biblical exegeses were definitive in his own day and remain authoritative in ours.

Perhaps this is enough for sainthood, but the man's character, especially as revealed in the incidents leading up to Hypatia's death, will always tarnish the admiration that these achievements should evoke.

It is of course natural that Damascius, as a pagan, should explicitly blame Cyril. This we may perhaps discount. But Socrates is usually interpreted as laying the guilt at the door of the monks of Nitria, Cyril's shock troops, whose power he subsequently fought to maintain. What little remains of Philostorgius's account is corroborative of this view.

If more needs to be said, let us take it from the mouth of Cyril's most vigorous defender, John of Nikiu: "[After Hypatia's death] all the people surrounded the patriarch Cyril and named him 'the new Theophilus'; for he had destroyed the last remains of idolatry in the city."

With this as the defense, what further need have we of witnesses?

# Chapter 8
# HYPATIA'S PHILOSOPHY

*N*o philosophical writing whatsoever of Hypatia's has come down to us, and indeed we have no record that she ever wrote on the subject, not at least for publication. Her (totally lost) letters to Synesius may well have commented on the philosophical works he sent her; indeed, we may safely assume that they did. But this is a very different matter from the preparation of more public documents. This has not prevented much speculation on the nature and content of her philosophical thought.

Socrates describes her philosophy by placing her in the tradition of Plato and Plotinus, although he errs in making the latter the head of a Neoplatonic school in Alexandria. We know that Plotinus studied in Alexandria, but his main teaching activity was conducted in Rome. It could be, however, that Alexandrian tradition liked to claim the famous Plotinus and that Hypatia was seen as working in that tradition.

Damascius has her "expounding in public on Plato or Aristotle or any other philosopher" and this has sometimes been interpreted to mean that her philosophy lectures were of a purely expository nature. Their popular character, vouched for most strongly by Damascius himself, leads one to think that they must have been more than that. True, Damascius compared Hypatia unfavorably with his own mentor, Isidorus, but he was writing over a century later and his was hardly an unbiased view to begin with. We shall see below that his denigration of Hypatia's geometric activities had a lot to do with his own opinions on the matter and that, adjoined to other evidence, it tells us something of Hypatia's own thought.

She was, of course, a woman, which Damascius at one point sees as a count against her, but his second charge, that she was a "mere geometer," is contradicted by other aspects of his own account. Besides, Hypatia herself had an admiring pupil, Synesius, and if we want to learn of her philosophy we will do best by examining his. Although this pupil left no *Life* of *his* teacher and the inferences we draw are thus less direct than we would like, his thought is closely linked to hers and the link is very well attested.

It is clear and undisputed that Synesius studied under Hypatia; moreover, he mentions no other teacher. His admiration for her is manifest and he sent various of his own writings to her for her opinion—the inference being that he saw in them reflections or developments of her own thought. As we shall see in chapter 9, he learned astronomy from her, and this makes it likely that he also studied the other branches of mathematics with her. The passage from his essay-letter *De Dono Astrolabii* quoted in chapter 6 not only extols the excellences of astronomy but includes as one of that science's virtues that its study involves both geometry and arithmetic, which he sees as above even astronomy in the hierarchy of scientific knowledge: giving "a fixed standard of truth." Elsewhere he writes of geometry as a "sacred" pursuit, and it would be odd indeed if this discipline and arithmetic too (both areas in which his teacher is known to have published) were not part of the study he undertook with Hypatia.

Hypatia's father, Theon, had a poor opinion of the geometric abilities of most of his students; his lectures on astronomy had had to be watered down to accommodate their meager skills. Synesius, by contrast, was able to design an astrolabe (though with Hypatia's help) and thus must have mastered the arithmetic and geometry necessary for this task. He may have written a (now lost) treatise on the astrolabe and one presumes this would have given the technical details he omitted from the surviving letter *De Dono Astrolabii*.

He wrote to Hypatia on this subject, enclosing a copy of *De Dono Astrolabii*, but long after its completion. This delay is not the case with the more overtly philosophical and speculative works he sent her: *Dion* and *On Dreams*. The latter has already been discussed in chapter 6; it is an attempt at a scientific work, although naturally it is much informed by its author's philosophical presuppositions. The former is straightforwardly a work of Neoplatonist philosophy. He most assuredly expected her approval for this work (indeed, he expressly sought it prior to its publication—the fact that it is extant means then that that approval was forthcoming) and thus we may be sure that it represents a strain of philosophical thought close to Hypatia's own.

The *Dion* is a systematic exposition of Synesius's philosophy, written at a time prior to his conversion to Christianity. It is very much a celebration of Hellenic culture—Hellenic culture in its entirety. That culture included the Greek language and its literature: a language and literature that Synesius knew intimately and cultivated assiduously— his writings absolutely brim over with literary allusions, citations, and direct quotations (which, incidentally, he must have expected his teacher to recognize and appreciate: we deduce that Hypatia herself was widely read). But that culture went beyond these aspects and included along with them the Greek religion as represented by the ideas of its greatest thinkers.

When Synesius later became a Christian, the form of Christianity he espoused was a highly Hellenized one. As a man of culture and status, he would never have been comfortable with the kerygmatic and simple faith of the first century. He would not have cast his lot with the working-class followers of the carpenter of Nazareth.

But it should equally be recognized that Synesius's Greek religion was not, as the Christians would have seen it, a worship of the false gods of the Olympian Pantheon. As already indicated in chapter 3, section B, there was a strain of Neoplatonist thought that stood apart, in large measure, from this popular tradition. The quest for mystic union with the One was not only a thoroughly Greek notion; it was at the same time a profoundly religious one. "They [certain barbarous men] have sacred hymns, holy symbols, and certain approaches to the Divine. But in reality all these things cut them off from the Divine. . . ."

This version of Greek religion, however, was not intrinsically at odds with Christianity. If one prescinded from the prejudices that Christians and pagans each held in respect of the other group, and listened instead to what was actually being *said*, then such a concept was not in any real conflict with Christian belief at all. A Christian, looking dispassionately at the notion of the One and its identification with the Good, contemplating the imperative it placed upon us to respond by seeking union with it via a pure and virtuous life, could hardly find such a religion repugnant. It need involve "no sacrifice nor [prayer] to any spirit" (to quote again Augustine) and thus was not inimical to Christian sensibilities.

Such a Christian, following such a course, would find Neoplatonist thought in this tradition not so much erroneous as incomplete. The Old and the New Testament offered direct revelation of God (the One), and this means of approach to the Godhead transcended the powers of unaided human reason, as used by the Neoplatonists, however lofty and inspired their ideas might be. In particular, the Christian would see the Neoplatonist as missing the central mystery of all true religion: the fact of the Incarnation.

Thus, when Synesius came to accept Christianity, he merely grafted these additional elements onto an already existing Neoplatonist stock. His Christianity remained an intellectual and Hellenist, indeed Neoplatonist, form of religion. He would, in essence, have been able to leave intact all his former religious mystique and merely assert in addition his acceptance of Jesus as his savior. Reading the Gospel of John, he would have found therein the Neoplatonist language so sympathetic to him: "At the beginning of time the Word already was; and God had the Word abiding with him, and the Word was God."

Synesius's version of Trinitarian doctrine (already prefigured in this passage) was a thoroughly Neoplatonist one with Greek rather than Hebrew antecedents. It is a much more intricate and elaborate one than the simple kerygmatic version outlined in chapter 3, section A. The account he developed, as described briefly in chapter 3, section C, was at once a more intellectual and a more mystical concept. It had clear Neoplatonist antecedents, deriving from Porphyry. It in no way conflicted with the simpler version—it merely extended and developed it.

In one matter in particular Synesius did find difficulty in accommodating to orthodox doctrine. He was, toward the end of his life, consecrated a bishop. It was a role he did not want, and indeed he sought to avoid it. In the first place he was married and did not want to leave his wife, as would normally have been required of him. (This matter of church discipline seems to have been solved by granting him a dispensation from the usual rules.) Second, he retained a belief in the preexistence of souls.

If Soul is held to be an emanation (either direct or indirect) of the One and if it is instantiated as individual (human) souls, then those souls are most consistently seen as being eternal, having neither beginning nor end. Orthodox Christian doctrine sees the matter differently. It takes the soul to be immortal, but assigns to it a definite temporal beginning. While each human body is formed naturally as a result of sexual intercourse, this does not explain the creation of a new human soul. At (or, as was held back then, some time after) conception, the fetus is specifically and individually "ensouled" by God as a special and particular act of creation, which makes God the father of us all.

This was the doctrine that Synesius had difficulty in accepting, as any thoroughgoing Neoplatonist would. However, Theophilus (Cyril's uncle), who was and remained Synesius's superior, overlooked the point and consecrated him anyway. This episode may explain why Synesius, who has always been seen as a significant theologian, hymnodist, and spiritual writer, has never been canonized.

The Neoplatonist philosophy that Synesius professed was the product of his study under Hypatia. It was not inimical to Christianity, despite its profoundly religious aspect. While it ignored, as a route to the One, the study of the Christian scriptures, it in no way denied them such a role, as the example of Synesius shows. A Christian, particularly a first-century Christian, would have found odd indeed the suggestion that mathematics was a route to God. Synesius did not; for him, geometry was "sacred" and he meant what he said. We may well therefore believe that Hypatia, too, held geometry to be sacred. The later Isidorus, who as we have seen "knew nothing of mathematics," would hardly preach a study of geometry as a route to the One, which is why Damascius saw Isidorus as a true philosopher and Hypatia as a "mere geometer."

That Hypatia's religious philosophy was not at odds with Christianity is deducible from the fact that she was not persecuted under Theophilus, whose character and views were otherwise much akin to those of his nephew Cyril. True, Hypatia did meet her death at Christian hands, but this was at least some twenty-five years after she began her public teaching. The bishop who razed the temple of Serapis took no action against Hypatia.

Thus, Theophilus must have seen no threat in Hypatia's teaching. Beyond this there may well have been a more direct factor operating in her favor. Improbable as it may seem, for the tolerant Synesius and the belligerent Theophilus were very different from one another, the two men were quite close. Theophilus solemnized Synesius's wedding and seems to have been instrumental in converting him to Christianity. Certainly he later prevailed upon him to take up a bishopric and indeed so consecrated him. Synesius addressed several of his extant letters to Theophilus and we have no hint of any breach between the two. This has puzzled a number of historians, but really there need be no inconsistency. Synesius may very well have foreseen that, with Christianity rapidly increasing its sway, the only future for his beloved Hellenic culture lay *within* Christianity—not in opposition to it. Theophilus, for his part, while he remained violently opposed to the worship of pagan gods, may well have looked on moderate pagans like Hypatia and on intermediaries such as Synesius as allies rather than as enemies. Even if in private he held stronger views, it may well have been expedient for him to support Synesius (and by implication, Hypatia) in public.

This is not to say that Synesius did not feel himself under some pressure in his compromise position. We may infer from a letter to Hypatia his desire to satisfy both the white-robed philosophers (pagans) and the dark ones (Christians). He continued to attempt and indeed to succeed in this balancing act. His conversion to Christianity no doubt gratified Theophilus, but it did not antagonize Hypatia.

Moreover, Synesius was adept in his cultivation of the ears of powerful men. He worked assiduously to acquire and to retain his influence through the good standing he held with them. (His gift of the astrolabe—crafted in silver by the best of smiths and accompanied by a specially composed essay-letter and possibly by a copy of a book— was bestowed upon one Paeonius and was explicitly designed to place himself high in that official's esteem.) Hypatia called Synesius "the providence of others" because he used his extensive network of powerful friends for others' benefit. (It worked both ways, of course: Synesius also asked Hypatia, one of his powerful friends via her friendship with, for example, Orestes, to assist two young men of his acquaintance. See appendix D, section D.5.)

While Synesius remained in good stead with Theophilus, the latter would certainly not move against the former's beloved teacher and soul mate. As long as Synesius and Theophilus retained their respective positions of influence and power, Hypatia was protected. Theophilus died in 412 and Synesius in 413. Hypatia was murdered in 415 or 416.

The justification advanced by those who committed this deed was, as we have seen, a misunderstanding or a misrepresentation of the true nature of her mathematical work. This misrepresentation would have allowed a further misrepresentation of her philosophical position. In truth, her philosophy, though of course not Christian, was not anti-Christian either. If Porphyry was the source of Synesius's Trinitarian mystique, and if Synesius learned his philosophy from Hypatia, then her instruction included Porphyrian concepts. However, Porphyry had written, in addition to his philosophical works, several anti-Christian polemics.

Trinitarian ideas of various types enter Neoplatonist thought most clearly with Plotinus, and were expounded also by Porphyry, although the details differ. Synesius's version is Porphyrian. His writings, brimful as they are with quotations and allusions to earlier works, do contain specific references to both these thinkers. But by far the most quoted philosopher is Plato himself. It is almost certainly from Plato that Synesius, and thus also Hypatia, derived their concept of the sacred nature of mathematics and its central position as a route to the One. This also suggests a reliance on Iamblichus, but here Synesius's references are vague allusions rather than confident direct quotes. It sounds as if Synesius, and by implication Hypatia, had had some report of Iamblichus's work but was not fully conversant with it.

It would seem, however, that in following Porphyry and, perhaps at a distance, Iamblichus, Hypatia and Synesius overlooked aspects of both these authors. They would hardly have accorded weight to Porphyry's anti-Christian polemics, and Iamblichus's theurgical enthusiasms would have been ignored. Neoplatonism was after all eclectic: one could pick and choose what aspects one adopted from any particular author.

The chief goal of Neoplatonist philosophy, as of course of Christianity, was the approach to the One. Both groups encouraged the celibate lifestyle (which Hypatia adopted) as well as the cultivation of the intellect and the power of the mind in the furtherance of this endeavor. However, for pagans of this persuasion the One was ineffable and in important ways unknowable. The Christian God also has this aspect, of course, but Christians also give another, familiar, face to God via the doctrine of the Incarnation, in the approachable and sympathetic person of Jesus of Nazareth. Thus the Christians claimed to know God in ways that Neoplatonists could readily dismiss as crude and vulgar—even blasphemous, much as many Muslims do today.

The central mystery of the One was to be approached but could never be mastered; one comes up against the limits of human knowledge. For some thinkers these limits come sooner than for others. At one extreme, one can despair of any certainty, but then it is, of course, inconsistent to claim to know merely that one can know nothing. However, a group known as the Cynics was influential in drawing attention to the limits of human knowledge. They were not a coherent school, any more than the Neoplatonist movement as a whole was coherent. However, they did develop a number of modes of unconventional, even outrageous, behavior that, in the mode of demonstration rather than of logic, of dialectic, or of rhetoric, advanced their cause in the eyes of those who witnessed such actions. One is rather reminded of the brief Western vogue of a version of Zen Buddhism in the 1970s.

There have been attempts to descry Cynic elements in Hypatia's teaching, and the obvious candidate is the menstrual napkin incident. This does indeed sound like a Cynic "demonstration," but this need not imply Cynic tendencies in Hypatia's philosophical outlook. The Cynics supplied mainstream philosophers with useful teaching techniques, but things need not have gone beyond that. Hypatia's interest and expertise in astronomy—the only truly successful empirical science of antiquity, the only one that could reliably predict the future—argues strongly against any idea that her philosophy put early limitations on the possibility of human knowledge. So, too, do her activities in the fields of "geometry and arithmetic, which it would not be improper to call a fixed standard of truth."

Those who lay stress on the Cynic elements in Hypatia's teaching suggest that her *tribon*, or academic robe, was in fact the rough cloak affected by the Cynics. This could be a further sign of a forsworn lifestyle, but the suggestion of an outward appearance of poverty sits ill with her riding in a carriage.

If one is prepared to deal in psychopathology, the removal of her cloak gives some perverted point to the action of her murderers in stripping her. This consideration applies whether in fact the *tribon* was a special Cynic "uniform" or merely the garb of an academic—one who in the normal course of events would be male. Figuratively, if not in actual fact, Hypatia wore the white robe of the pagan scholar, not the dark robe of the Christian.

Whatever flimsy pretext her murderers may have advanced, the especially brutal aspects evident in her slaying owe much of their motivation to Hypatia's womanhood and to sheer lust on the part of the perpetrators. Some accounts of her death have been dismissed as sado-erotic, but the charge is more properly directed to the murderers themselves. It is difficult to find any philosophical motive beyond the most slender of pretexts for their action.

# Chapter 9
# HYPATIA'S MATHEMATICS

*A*lthough we may reconstruct aspects of Hypatia's philosophy with some confidence, we are much better placed when we come to her mathematics. We are told explicitly of three of her mathematical publications, and we have indications of yet more.

## A. BACKGROUND AND SOURCES

The two greatest works of the Alexandrian mathematical tradition are undoubtedly Euclid's *Elements* and Ptolemy's *Almagest*.

The first of these is a text on geometry, but includes much of what we would now refer to as algebra or arithmetic. The geometry considers the two simplest of the plane (two-dimensional) figures, the straight line and the circle, together with their properties, both separately and together. It later continues to three-dimensional analogues, the plane, the cylinder, the cone, and the sphere. The *Elements* constitute a definitive account of what was known in relation to this subject matter, and it became the archetypal statement of this area of knowledge.

The second work occupies a similar place in the development of astronomy. Just as Euclid's masterpiece rendered obsolete all that had preceded it and came to supersede the older works, so, too, did

Ptolemy's account supplant earlier work in its field, in particular that of Hipparchus.

Thus, these two books between them represented the best of the Alexandrian mathematical tradition, and together constituted a definitive summary of a great deal of it. It was precisely on this account, surely, that Hypatia's father, Theon, spent much of his time and effort on these works. It was Theon's edition of Euclid that for many years was our only means of access to the *Elements*, and his commentary on the *Almagest* has likewise been an important source for later editors. (Ptolemy also produced a companion volume, the *Handy Tables*, and this was also given much attention by Theon.)

Theon's work constituted a major piece of conservation of ancient knowledge, undertaken at a time when the tradition that had produced it was under severe threat. However, important as these works were, they did not summarize the entire Alexandrian mathematical tradition.

In the area of geometry, later work had gone beyond the material treated in the *Elements*. If, in three dimensions, a plane and a cone are placed together, they will intersect one another, and the planar (two-dimensional) curve along the intersection is a new type of curve, neither a straight line nor a circle (except in a few very special cases). This new type of curve is termed a "conic section" because of the way in which it is generated. Quite frequently, the name is abbreviated to simply "conic." There are three different types of conic: the *ellipse* (an oval figure, with the circle as a special case), the *parabola*, and the *hyperbola*.

Euclid produced a work on *Conics*, but this was superseded by a later (and probably fuller) treatment by Apollonius. Apollonius's work, then, was the best treatment available of this later extension of geometric knowledge. Other aspects of the *Elements* dealt with what we would now consider algebra or arithmetic. In this area also there had been major developments since Euclid. Here the principal author was Diophantus, who is regarded as the founder of a branch of mathematics today called number theory. It is now viewed as a branch of algebra, but Diophantus's work is still referred to as the *Arithmetic*.

(Even today, there is a vogue for the term "higher arithmetic" for number theory.)

Between them, Apollonius and Diophantus represented the best later Alexandrian mathematics. Thus a summary of the entire mathematical corpus would contain their work in addition to that of Euclid and Ptolemy. It is precisely to these areas of mathematics that Hypatia directed her attention. This is what we shall concentrate on for most of this chapter, although there are other matters that we must also consider.

As we have seen, many of the primary sources attest that Hypatia was a mathematician, and some even give a vague indication as to the branches of mathematics that she practiced, describing her as a geometer or as an astronomer. However, very few descriptions provide more precise detail.

Of these the most direct is Theon's inscription at the start of Book III of his Commentary on Ptolemy's *Almagest*. There is considerable discussion as to its exact significance, and the various possibilities will be discussed in more detail in section B. However, there is universal agreement that it implies collaboration of some sort between father and daughter.

The *Suda Lexicon* tells us that Hypatia wrote three books. The relevant passage is precisely twelve words long and the text is corrupt, with misspellings, probable deletions, and different manuscripts suggesting different meanings. The excerpt has therefore been the subject of various alternative and disputed readings. Nonetheless, there is today a general consensus that Paul Tannery, a nineteenth-century historian of mathematics and science, has given the correct rendering: "She wrote a Commentary on Diophantus, [one on] the astronomical *Canon*, and a Commentary on Apollonius's *Conics*."

These works will be considered in the later sections of this chapter (see sections B–F). I will discuss the astronomical work first, and then look at the geometric and arithmetic works.

We also learn of her mathematical and scientific work from surviving letters of Synesius. His sending to her copies of his *Dion* and

*On Dreams* has already been discussed for their philosophical import, and we need say no more of these, for the "science" of the latter requires no further notice; by today's standards it can hardly merit the name.

In a different category, however, are references to her work on the astrolabe, which will require more careful treatment and consideration, and a letter describing a "hydroscope," asking her to have one made for him.

These matters will also be discussed in this chapter (see sections G and H), but they are less important to the overall picture we form of her than are the areas mentioned in the *Suda*.

Finally, various attempts have been made to attribute yet other works to Hypatia. For the most part these attributions are unsupported and will be ignored. However, it is important to consider carefully the best and most detailed such attempt, that of the twentieth-century historian Wilbur Richard Knorr.

Knorr begins his analysis by considering passages from Book III of Theon's Commentary on the *Almagest*, in which Hypatia had some hand, and comparing them with similar passages in Book I, which is stated to be Theon's alone. Then, finding certain differences of style, he looks for evidences of these two styles throughout the remainder of the commentary and deduces Hypatia's influence on, in particular, Book IV. He next goes on to consider various other mathematical works and finds evidence of her hand in four other places. Because the list of works given in the *Suda* is usually read as failing to mention the work attested by Theon, he feels confident that this list is incomplete. This point will be discussed further in sections E and I of this chapter and in chapter 10.

Knorr's work is avowedly speculative and is by no means universally accepted. Indeed, it is a matter of some controversy. However, it merits careful consideration, and we will look at it in some detail in sections B, C, D, and I of this chapter.

# B. BOOK III OF THE *ALMAGEST*

The work we now refer to as the *Almagest* was originally named the *Mathematike Syntaxis*, which is to say the "Mathematical [i.e., in this context, Astronomical] Collection." It came to be known by a couple of informal names, probably to distinguish it from an earlier "astronomical collection." One of these names was *E Megiste Syntaxis* ("The Greatest Collection"). This name was adopted in transliteration as *al-majisti* by later Arab translators and later rendered as the Latin *Almagestum*, the name that has stuck.

The work in question is the key exposition of Ptolemy's version of the solar system and its motion. It remained influential from the date of its writing for many centuries thereafter, to the time of Copernicus, Kepler, and Galileo, supplanting all that had gone before it. Pappus wrote a commentary on it as also did Theon. It was a thoroughgoing work on the theory of the solar system and eminently suited for use as a textbook because it assumed no prior knowledge of astronomy, merely familiarity with Euclid's geometry. Even the relevant arithmetic was taught within its pages.

The usual interpretation of the inscription ("the recension of my philosopher-daughter Hypatia") to the extant version of Theon's Commentary on Book III is that its source is a second edition of this work, supplanting an earlier one by Theon alone. On this reading, Theon, recognizing his daughter's improvement on his own earlier work, replaced his version with hers.

This interpretation has been disputed. Another reading has Hypatia merely editing the text of Ptolemy's work and her father providing the passages of comment. This is, however, a less widely held view and thus I have accepted the opinion that some of Hypatia's writing survives in our present text.

There have been various printings of Theon's Commentary. In the nineteenth century, the Abbé Halma produced a version, but the more recent edition by Professor A. Rome is much to be preferred. Rome suggested the methodology whereby the section attributed, at least in part, to Hypatia (i.e., Book III) should be compared in detail for points of style with those other passages (Books I and II) credited directly to Theon. He embarked upon such a project, exploring a number of possible avenues, but without reaching any definite conclusion.

Rome might well have gone further with this work but for the difficult conditions under which he labored. His research was conducted in Nazi-occupied Belgium during World War II and many of his notes were destroyed. This hampered the edition he prepared and also, if one reads between the lines, ended any idea he may have had of writing a life of Hypatia to supplant the fanciful and sentimental account given by Halma.

Rome did, however, draw attention to one important thing. This was that the method employed in a long division performed in Book III (on the sun) differed from that explained in Book I (on mathematical technique). The method in Book III employs a tabular approach, whereas the one in Book I does not; this latter is less systematic and in fact inferior. For the technical detail, see appendix A; however, it is appropriate to remark that a tabular approach is much closer to later versions of the long division algorithm, and represents a clear improvement over that outlined in Theon's Commentary on Book I. What we are dealing with here is efficiency of computational technique, and, although the long division algorithms occur in an astronomical context, they are of a more general application than this.

Knorr, accepting Rome's implication that the improved technique was due to Hypatia, examined the style of the two passages on long division, looking for differences in the modes of expression employed. This led him to notice systematic divergences not only in vocabulary and in grammar (for details of which the reader is referred to his book) but also of overall style.

Generally speaking, it is considered a mark of good style to vary the mode of expression as one proceeds from one element to another in an otherwise repetitive list. Instead of writing:

> First apply Procedure A to the number B to find the answer C;
> Next apply Procedure A to the number C to find the answer D;
> Next apply Procedure A to the number D to find the answer E; etc.

we might instead say:

> Begin by applying Procedure A to the number B and thus obtain the answer C; repeat the application but using C in place of B, and so determine a second answer D; continuing in this manner using D as the operand, find a further result E; and so on.

However, in certain contexts, and I would say that this is one of them, the first style is to be preferred to the second. Its strophic, formulaic character suits instruction in the performance of a repetitive computational process.

Knorr associates the first style with Hypatia and the second with Theon. Thus armed, he sets out to discover Hypatian influence in other texts that may have passed through her hands.

Before we follow him, however, we may note that Hypatia in all probability *did* value good prose style. Synesius complained to her: "Some of those who wear the white or dark mantle have maintained that I am faithless to philosophy, apparently because I profess a grace and harmony of style." As Knorr remarks, "It is clear that he expects a sympathetic audience from Hypatia."

Despite his attention to his writing, Theon was not a stylist. As Rome observes: "Theon is not a stylist, but he knows how to say accurately and clearly what he wants." Evidently Hypatia went further but, like all good stylists, knew when rules should be broken.

## C. BOOKS IV–XIII OF THE *ALMAGEST*

The obvious place to begin a search for further writings by Hypatia is in the remaining, unattributed books (IV–XIII) of Theon's Commentary on the *Almagest*. In this body of work, long division also appears: in Book IV, which is devoted to the moon, and in Book IX, which begins the study of the planets.

The approach adopted in Book IV is the same as that in Book III. Not only is a table set up and used, but the style is the same. Knorr's inference is that this passage also comes from Hypatia's pen.

The case is different when we come to the calculation in Book IX. In this instance, although a table is used, we find neither the same style of presentation nor the clarity of exposition. The conclusion is that Hypatia is not the author of this part of the work.

The reader will hardly fail to notice the speculative nature of the argument employed here. At one point in his detective classic *The Hound of the Baskervilles*, Arthur Conan Doyle has his hero, Sherlock Holmes, deny the charge of guesswork by the claim that he is entering "the region where we balance probabilities and choose the most likely." This is Knorr's method, and we are not finished with it. It will resurface in sections D and I, below.

It should be noted that the method has not gone unchallenged. One critic, Alan Cameron, not only disagrees with the textual basis (the translation of Theon's inscription) but also with the manner in which the subsequent argument is constructed. Cameron has the labor of Book III being divided in the sense that it is "the *commentary* of Theon, with the *edition* [i.e., interpolated text] revised by . . . Hypatia." He sees Hypatia as performing the more menial task of preparing text (for Books III–XIII) and not providing commentary. He also takes issue with other aspects of the methodology and concludes that "no confidence can be placed in any attempt to reconstruct Hypatia in this way."

This seems to me to overlook the clear similarities in the division algorithms of Books III and IV and the manifest difference from the approach of Book I. It seems eminently plausible that Hypatia's hand may be seen not only in Book III but also in Book IV. But whether we follow Knorr in his even more speculative suggestions or instead take heed of Cameron's voice of caution is probably a matter of individual preference.

# D. APOLLONIUS'S *CONICS*

The curves known as "conic sections" (or "conics" for short) are, as their name implies, those produced by taking a cross section of a cone, that is, a "cut" in the cone, or equivalently, its intersection with a plane. Depending on how the cut is made, various possibilities arise. The standard cone is the familiar "witch's hat" shape and this is what is employed in modern accounts. However, the cone envisaged by Apollonius was somewhat more general and can be, and in fact usually is, pushed somewhat sideways, so that the apex is typically off center. The details are given in appendix A; we need only pause here to note that three different cases arise, depending on how far this point is displaced from the central axis. Of these three, one is a special case; the other two are more general.

Apollonius's *Conics* comprises eight books, of which only the first seven survive in close to their entirety. Books I–IV have come down to us in the Greek via a commentary by Eutocius, who was active as a mathematician in the early sixth century. Books V–VII reach us through Arabic translations. It is regarded as probable that Eutocius's *Commentary* embraced only the first four books, and this is usually suggested as the reason for our lack of a full Greek text.

These first four books form a general introduction to the subject and develop the elementary properties of the cone and the conic sections. Much of this work was already known prior to Apollonius (e.g., to Euclid and to Archimedes), but Apollonius's treatment came to be recognized as superior to anything that preceded it. Even these elementary parts of his treatise contained original material.

The *Suda* tells us that Hypatia wrote a commentary on Apollonius's *Conics*, but it does not say whether all the books were included or only the first four. No direct copy of her work survives. However, one possibility is that Eutocius, in preparing his own commentary, had access to it (along with other such material).

Knorr explored this possibility in respect to one set of passages occurring early in Book I. Of the three cases referred to above, the first (special) case is rather easier than the other two. The others are in fact similar to one another in many respects. Knorr makes a detailed comparison of the wording in these two comparable cases. His conclusion is that the discussion of the second case is a composite text, written by an author using a Euclidean text of two subsidiary but related theorems, but revised by an editor without direct access to that text. He proposed that the author was Hypatia, the editor Eutocius.

If we make allowance for the likely editorial changes, we find parallel exposition of the two cases: each is treated in detail, as if to reinforce concepts, rather than to leave some matters to the student. Modern authors use such devices as "Similarly for Case 3," "Case 3 follows *mutatis mutandis*," "The detailed discussion of Case 3 is left as an exercise for the student," and so forth, and such devices were also available then. However, this practice was not followed in this case, and this may indicate a teacher cum textbook-writer conscious of the need to spell such matters out in full detail for the benefit of weaker students. If this writer was Hypatia, then this picture fits exactly with the other glimpses we have of her as a teacher of mathematics.

# E. THE ASTRONOMICAL *CANON*

The text of the *Suda* at the point where Hesychius lists Hypatia's writings is unfortunately corrupt and earlier writers spent some time and effort in discussing what was actually meant. However, the version given in this book in appendix D, section A.1 (and quoted in section A of this chapter), follows a suggestion by Tannery and is now rarely if ever questioned.

If we accept this rendering, we find that Hypatia is credited with a commentary on "the Astronomical *Canon*," that is, "The Astronomical Table." Now we have seen that she was involved in preparing, at least an edition of, more likely a commentary on, Ptolemy's *Almagest*. It is possible that this is the work Hesychius had in mind, but this is far from certain.

If it was her commentary on that work that he was referring to, he would perhaps more likely have called it by its Greek name, the *Syntaxis*. The most obvious author on whom a later writer might comment remains Ptolemy. Ptolemy, having written the *Almagest*, extracted from it various of the tables it contained—tables required for the making of astronomical calculations. He issued these separately, together with an introduction, as a new work titled *Procheiroi Canones*, the *Handy Tables*.

In addition to his Commentary on the *Almagest*, Hypatia's father, Theon, wrote two separate commentaries on this derivative work. These are known respectively as the *Large Commentary* and the *Small Commentary*," the first having been written before the second. The latter was edited (as is now agreed, very badly) in the version produced by Abbé Halma in 1822. Halma, in fact, attributed the work to Hypatia in his *Discours Préliminaire*, although not in his title. His grounds for this attribution begin with the *Suda* passage, but otherwise strike me as being in large part sentimental. Certainly the later and more scholarly editor Anne Tihon discounts this suggestion. Nor has there ever been any hint of a trace of Hypatia's hand in Theon's *Large Commentary*.

This makes for a puzzle, for if Hypatia produced a now lost commentary on the *Handy Tables*, this would mean that between them, father and daughter wrote three commentaries on this one book, which seems rather excessive. Theon's *Small Commentary* was produced to meet the needs of those weaker students who could not follow all the material in the other. However, there would seem no need for yet another commentary.

There is perhaps a different solution to this dilemma. This is to reject Tannery's suggested interpolation and to go back to the reading espoused by an earlier historian, Jean Baptiste Joseph Delambre, whose 1817 version would incline us to reconstruct Hesychius's passage as: "She wrote a commentary on Diophantus, the astronomical table, and a commentary on Apollonius's *Conics*."

The way is now open for us to interpret the "astronomical table" as the tabular method of long division, introduced in her version of Book III of the *Almagest*. True, a new method (or more accurately a revised and more systematic approach to an older method) of long division is not necessarily astronomical, but the context in which it is presented most definitely is, and the innovation consists precisely in the construction of a table.

# F. THE *ARITHMETIC* OF DIOPHANTUS

Diophantus was a most original mathematician whose work is seen as central in the development of algebra, not least for its influence on later mathematicians. Of the various works he is known to have written, only a small portion survives, but that which does is sufficient to demonstrate his technical ability and his originality. His major work is his *Arithmetic*, for us perhaps a somewhat misleading name. It is closer in spirit to aspects of what today we would call algebra, or more technically "number theory." More specifically it is seen as initiating a branch of number theory now named in his honor: diophantine analysis.

One of mathematics' most famous problems, which has only recently yielded up a proof, is the so-called Fermat's Last Theorem. This is a problem in diophantine analysis that was first stated by the seventeenth-century amateur (but very great) mathematician Pierre de Fermat as a direct result of his reading of Diophantus.

Originally, the *Arithmetic* comprised thirteen books, each a collection of problems posed and solved. Of this only a portion has come down to us. Various hypotheses have been advanced as to the status of that fragment that survives in the Greek. Until recently, the consensus was that the six surviving books were the first six and that the final seven were missing. This view was first proposed by Tannery, who further suggested that what had in fact survived was Hypatia's Commentary, which he presumed extended only to the first six books. This idea was advanced in emulation of the one that sees the first four books of Apollonius's *Conics*, and only these, as surviving in the original Greek because that was the extent of Eutocius's Commentary.

Tannery's hypothesis was widely accepted. However, it was even more complicated than I have so far outlined. It involved the production of a detailed, if in part speculative, "family tree" connecting the known Greek manuscripts. This family tree was modified in one point by the later historian Sir Thomas Heath, when he produced his English translation of the *Arithmetic*.

So the question could be asked: if the surviving books had passed through Hypatia's hands, then was it possible to identify what was hers and not a part of Diophantus's original? This was not seen, however, as a question admitting any easy answer, for Tannery and Heath also posited that at some stage a later scribe had attempted to restore the original text, and thus (from our point of view) muddied the waters: "[But] the distinction between text and scholia being sometimes difficult to draw, he included a good deal which should have been left out." Thus, although according to this once popular account there had been a systematic attempt to delete Hypatian addenda, some might in fact have survived.

Heath and others made considerable attempts to identify those parts of the extant Greek text that would seem to be interpolations. The clearest case would seem to be the first seven problems of Book II. Of these, Problems 1–5 in essence repeat material from Book I. Problems 6 and 7 were judged by Tannery (on stylistic grounds) to be later additions.

This pair of problems reads very much like a couple of student exercises. One has the impression of a student text in which we pause before commencing a more advanced topic: pause first to revise work previously undertaken and pause again to flex the mathematical muscles a little on a pair of new but straightforward examples.

If this material is due to Hypatia, then it is quite compatible with what the sources lead us to believe of her—that she was greatly revered as a *teacher*. There is also a further possible connection: in the treatment of Problem II.7, a nine-word phrase in the original Greek is identical with one in Euclid's *Data* that her father had edited.

This entire story, however, contains certain implausible elements that have been recognized all the more because recent discoveries have shown the basic premises to be mistaken. Four more books of Diophantus's *Arithmetic* have since come to light, these having been discovered in Arabic translation and subsequently published. They turn out to correspond to Books IV–VII of Diophantus's original. Thus the books previously known as IV, V, and VI (now referred to as "IV," etc.) must be three of the remaining six books (VIII–XIII), although it is a matter of some debate which three.

But comparison of the Greek and the Arabic texts reveals enormous stylistic differences. The Greek is sparse and to the point, whereas the Arabic is prolix and repetitive. In particular, the Arabic version concludes each problem with a check that the answer is indeed correct and then for good measure adds a recapitulation of the work done. Both these elements are absent from the Greek.

It thus follows that it is the Arabic, rather than the Greek, books that have undergone major revision. So if one text or the other is to be sourced to a commentary, then that source is likely to be preserved in the Arabic rather than in the Greek.

But now the only author known to have produced so early a commentary is Hypatia, so the suggestion now is that if Hypatia's work survives, then it is preserved in the Arabic and not, as previously assumed, in the Greek. The most obvious hypothesis is that the novel elements (or at least some part of these) found in the Arabic and not in the Greek are due to Hypatia. It should, however, be said at once that by no means does all current scholarship entertain this possibility.

One reason for this reluctance is that the addenda say virtually nothing of any real mathematical significance, and hence "[r]etrieving the commentator via stylistic comparisons of the Arabic and Greek texts would thus isolate an essentially trivial mind." Which, of course, is something that, in the face of other evidence, we are reluctant to attribute to Hypatia.

Such a view may, however, be a trifle hasty. From the viewpoint of those who advance mathematics at the research level, the efforts of popularizers and of pedagogues are seen as trivial and, indeed, both these terms are not infrequently used in a pejorative sense. This is unfair, of course, and indeed few would, in the cold light of day, argue for so uncompromising a view so baldly stated.

Hypatia's father, Theon, was hardly a research mathematician; he taught, edited, commented on, preserved, and supplied minor addenda to the works of other much greater mathematicians. He lived at a time when scholarship was under threat and the priority lay in the preservation of knowledge. He had cause, as we have already seen, to complain about the poor background of his students. Nonetheless, his work survives, and his name lives on because he did the job of preservation well. Today's mathematics is much in his debt.

This matter will be considered in greater depth in chapter 10, which will also offer the hypothesis that in her scholarly priorities Hypatia was very much her father's daughter. She was anxious to preserve the mathematical classics of the past and to teach them to a new generation of students—students who were, in the main, none too bright. If one writes for such readers, then one *does* feel the need to dot every *i* and to cross every *t*, however tedious such an enterprise may be.

Theon at times wrote like this; if Hypatia's writing is preserved in the early passage of Eutocius's Commentary on Apollonius, then so, in another context, did she. Quite possibly she also did so here. Her scholia may in fact have consisted of the preparation (or the supervision) of checks on Diophantus's answers. Thus it is currently seen as most likely that she produced the checks, but that the final summaries are the work of some later hand.

Even today, mathematics teachers insist that students, having solved a problem, then check their solution lest an error has occurred. In most cases this is mathematically trivial, but pedagogically it is sound advice. To publish the results need not so much evidence a "trivial mind" in oneself as recognize it in those one is constrained to teach.

## G. THE ASTROLABE

There were two distinct instruments that are sometimes referred to as "astrolabes." Think of the sky as an enormous sphere on which are projected the various constellations and their unchanging relationships to one another. This is called the "celestial sphere" by astronomers even today. Against this, the moon and planets were seen to move. Among the various constellations represented on this celestial sphere are, in particular, the different signs or "houses" of the zodiac, twelve in all. The sun is also to be thought of as passing through these houses; this cannot be observed directly, but the positions of its rising and setting tell us in which house it is located at different times of the year.

The first type of astrolabe is now more precisely known as the "armillary sphere." This comprised a model of the celestial sphere. The earth's axis may be envisaged as being extended and passing through the celestial sphere at points known as the north and south celestial poles, the first of which is the approximate position of the star Polaris. The circle connecting all the points equidistant between these poles is the celestial equator. The celestial poles and the celestial equator are represented by parts of the armillary sphere.

The armillary sphere was thus a material replica of some aspects of the celestial sphere, comprising various circles representing the celestial equator, the ecliptic (the apparent path of the sun through the heavens), various lines of latitude and longitude, and possibly a plumb line to adjust the device to the local horizontal. (See plate 1.)

An armillary sphere could be set up with its "equator" parallel to the real equator and with its axis parallel to that of the earth (as the gnomon of a sundial is so aligned), and then used to determine, for example, the day of the equinox, when the shadow cast by the upper half of the instrument's "equator" exactly covered the lower half. Other observations could also be made, sometimes with the aid of holes drilled in the metal circles, or by means of graduated scales carried upon them.

Armillary spheres came in a wide range of sizes from large instruments that, in essence, constituted parts of ancient observatories, to small handheld models that were in effect instructional toys. The large ones achieved accuracy and practicality at the expense of being unwieldy and not easily portable, but they could be adapted to a variety of uses as clocks, calendars, and computational aids.

A considerable advance was the discovery that the same ends could be achieved by means of a flat, circular instrument comprising various pieces of metal with lines engraved upon them and able to move with respect to one another. This instrument was at first called the "little astrolabe" to distinguish it from the armillary sphere, which also went by the name *astrolabon*. The theory that allowed the perspective rendering of the various portions of the armillary sphere on one or another of the various flat surfaces of the (little) astrolabe is known as "stereographic projection," and it was known to Ptolemy, and quite possibly to the earlier astronomer Hipparchus (as attested by Synesius in *De Dono Astrolabii*). In its simplest form, the astrolabe (this term came to be standard for the smaller, flat instrument) consisted of an engraved circular metal base, the *mater*, a circular metal web, or *rete*, and a sighting rod, or *alidade*, all held together with a pin. (See plates 2 and 3.) The engravings on the mater were specific to a particular location (or, more precisely, specific latitude), but if one expected to travel to other places, then the mater could be overlaid by other engraved plates, known as *climates*, and placed between the mater and the rete. Thus the instrument could also be used as a navigational aid, not unlike the later sextant in some of its uses.

The theory of stereographic projection was given by Ptolemy in his *Planisphaerium*, a work that also includes tabular material. Later astronomers credited Ptolemy with works on both the armillary sphere and the "little astrolabe." Others credit Theon with works on these same topics, and the most likely explanation is that he produced commentaries on the earlier works of Ptolemy.

Theon's two works on the astrolabe (in both its forms) are now lost as originals, but there are grounds for the suggestion that they are partially preserved as the common source of several later works, some of which very likely present parts of them in translation (into Arabic and Syriac). Thus, Theon was conserving earlier knowledge here also, albeit that his efforts were here less effective than in the case of his work with the *Elements* and the *Almagest*.

Synesius, in his letter to Paeonius (*De Dono Astrolabii*), tells how he himself designed the astrolabe, which he is presenting to that worthy, but with help from Hypatia, and then had it crafted by the very best of silversmiths. The letter contains some material on the theory of the astrolabe, and for the most part seems to indicate that it is the "little astrolabe," that is, the flat instrument, that is in question. The inference is that Theon passed on his knowledge to his daughter and that she in her turn taught Synesius. If, as some have suggested, Synesius produced a longer monograph on the theory, a more technical work than the surviving letter, this must have been lost.


# H. THE "HYDROSCOPE"

The other instrument of which Synesius writes to Hypatia is the "hydroscope." This name is a direct transliteration of the Greek, and although there is a detailed description of the instrument, there was once much discussion of what the device actually was and what was its use. Various suggestions were advanced, but the matter may now be regarded as resolved, at least as far as the first question is concerned.

It was the mathematician Fermat (the same man encountered in section F above) who put forward the suggestion, now universally accepted, that the device was a hydrometer, that is to say a densimeter for use in liquids. (See plate 4.) This is the only interpretation that makes sense of the detailed description of the instrument. (For an English translation of the text, see appendix D, section D.2.) Once this meaning is advanced, it is at once apparent that no other interpretation is possible. From the tone of the letter, especially its opening sentence, "I am in such evil fortune that I need a hydroscope," it is generally supposed that Synesius is writing from his sickbed, indeed, on the modern dating of the letters, from his deathbed. It was formerly supposed that the hydrometer was to be employed to test the quality of his drinking water or perhaps of some liquid medicine or other. Another possibility is that he was *making* some sort of medicine for himself, possibly by fermentation or distillation.

However, a further possibility has recently been suggested. This is that the hydrometer was specifically a urinometer, such as is still used (occasionally) today. The specific gravity (i.e., the density) of urine could be measured to calculate the required dose of some diuretic. This would suggest that Synesius suffered from either renal disease, mature onset diabetes mellitus, or possibly cardiac failure. Any one of these diagnoses would be compatible with his death shortly after this letter was written.

W. S. Crawford, an earlier commentator on Synesius, makes the remark that, in writing to Hypatia and describing the hydroscope in some detail, he is assuming that she does not already know of the instrument. He does, however, trust her, indeed relies on her, to follow his meaning and to have the device constructed. *We* may further remark that his somewhat terse description puzzled commentators for some twelve hundred years, but presumably did not cause Hypatia any trouble. Synesius clearly took the view that a basic outline would suffice and that his teacher could supply the details.

## I. OTHER WORK

There have from time to time been suggestions of other works from Hypatia's hand. In the main, we may discount these. However, Knorr's stylistic analysis led him to propose that she in fact edited some other mathematical works. The most important of these is Archimedes' *Dimension of the Circle*. This comes to us via a Greek version that he calls DC, as well as in several translations into Latin. These latter appear to derive from a common source, which is not, however, DC, but must be a lost Greek version. This he calls DC*, and his suggestion is that this edition is Hypatia's.

In part, this suggestion derives from the likely date of DC*, in part from an analysis of the style employed. The argument is technical and somewhat inconclusive, and Knorr admits to certain difficulties with it. However, it does possess a certain plausibility.

Two other works he also cites as showing possible influence of Hypatian edition. These are an anonymous tract *On Isoperimetric Figures* and a short geometric work *De Curvis Superficiebus* (On Curved Surfaces).

Isoperimetric figures are flat shapes having a prescribed perimeter. If we ask which of these contains the largest area, the answer is a circle, but there are many other results as well. For example, if we direct our attention to regular figures like the equilateral triangle, the square, the equal-sided pentagon, hexagon, and so forth, then there is a result to the effect that the more sides there are the larger the area, and there are other such results.

*De Curvis Superficiebus* is concerned with the geometry of the sphere, the cylinder, and the cone. Its authorship is disputed, and although it is believed to derive from a Greek original, it is known only in Latin translation.

In both these cases Knorr posits lost manuscripts AI* and CS* that came from Hypatia's hand, so that some of her work is also preserved in modern versions of these works.

That these works, if hers, are not listed by Hesychius need not surprise us. The three works he lists are either commentaries or (possibly in the case of the Astronomical *Canon*) original works. The other possible attributions are *editions*, where her own contribution would be considerably less. He might well not have seen these as coming into the category of truly original works.

All in all, however, and rather sadly, whatever the full extent of her writing, very little of it has come down to us, and anything we do have is almost never in its original form.

# Chapter 10

# EVALUATION

The almost universally agreed assessment of Theon's achievement is that, in overall terms, he was a minor mathematician. He was, however and most definitely, a specialist mathematician and astronomer, and so when he is described as a "philosopher" (e.g., in the *Suda*), then that word is used in the generic sense of "thinker" or "academic." He did not, although his daughter did, interest himself in the speculative areas of (religious) philosophy, but confined himself rather to the technical aspects of his craft.

He was in his day the foremost mathematician in the Roman Empire, very likely in the world. Even this is not to say that he was a great mathematician as these things are commonly judged. Euclid was a great mathematician in that he systematized the knowledge of previous researchers and set a standard of presentation and of exposition that persists to this day. Euclid in large part defined the mathematical agenda.

Theon is remembered, more than for anything else, for the role he played in preserving the text of Euclid's major work, the *Elements*. This is an important part to have played in the history of mathematics. We are very much in Theon's debt; without him we would know less of Euclid's work.

But it is important to distinguish the nature of Euclid's work from that of Theon's. The first man was a major contributor, the second a preserver of preexisting knowledge. We may make a similar point in relation to Theon's Commentaries on Ptolemy. Ptolemy was a major innovator and researcher. Theon was not; he explained the work of his predecessor to (mostly none-too-bright) students, and so sought to render potentially difficult concepts accessible. This is a not dishonorable task, but it is a subsidiary and derivative one. Without Ptolemy's *Almagest*, there could be no commentary of Theon.

Theon's contribution to our mathematical knowledge has long been agreed to have been this: that he has attained importance above his actual mathematical abilities because of the key part his work has played in the preservation of earlier mathematical classics.

It can often sound as a harsh judgment so to label a figure such as Theon. One even finds from time to time a hint of disapproval of Theon and such pedagogues, when they are compared to the giants of the mathematical pantheon: the Euclids and the Ptolemies of this world. Of course the latter are the greater; they are the original thinkers and we rightly celebrate them. But this should not involve us in the denigration of the also valuable if more humble role played by the Theons and their ilk.

One should also bear in mind the times in which Theon worked: turbulent, in many ways anti-intellectual. The Museum was dying and the libraries were either gone or in process of destruction. The great classics of the past, the glories of Alexandria's mathematical tradition, the works of Euclid and Ptolemy—all were under threat of permanent oblivion. Theon's major work was to preserve the classic expositions of these great figures from the past.

We can see the thrust of his life's work as being the production of his editions of and commentaries on these acknowledged masterpieces. He taught from them, and so, both in writing and in the living minds of his pupils, he sought to preserve the heritage of Alexandria and its mathematics. It was, as I have already remarked in chapter 6, an endeavor not unlike today's "Great Books" programs.

When we come to Hypatia, we find Philostorgius stating that she greatly outshone her father. Perhaps a similar judgment is implied by Damascius, who bases his judgment on her eminence as a philosopher (in the narrow sense) as well as in her capacity as a mathematician. Socrates speaks of her as surpassing the attainments of her contemporaries, although he may not have had Theon in mind. However, Theon's inscription at the beginning of Book III of his Commentary on the *Almagest* may lead us to infer that he regarded her version as an improvement on his own. Certainly it is often so interpreted.

This last, to my mind, is the action of a proud father: suppressing his own work in favor of a manifest improvement by his daughter. The new method of long division, a matter of computational technique and efficiency (important then as now), was a clear advance and Theon recognized the point.

It thus makes sense to regard Hypatia as surpassing her father, not so much as a mathematician (although some popular works adopt this position uncritically) but as a teacher of the subject. When it comes to the written works that might assist our judgment, however, we are poorly placed. For this would be the only way to make a truly independent judgment; anything else is hearsay.

The major Alexandrian classics of the early period were precisely the ones that Theon preserved. His daughter continued this work, but the originals that *she* made the subject of her commentaries were later and more difficult works: the *Conics* of Apollonius and the *Arithmetic* of Diophantus. This can quite readily be viewed as a simple extension of a scholarly program initiated by her father. Euclid's *Elements* is, however, a textbook, indeed a textbook par excellence, and it even remains in (limited) use as such today. Ptolemy's *Almagest*, proceeding as it does from first principles, may also be regarded as a textbook, although it may simultaneously be looked upon as an exposition of research.

This "textbook" orientation is not at all as readily apparent in, say, Diophantus's *Arithmetic*. Diophantus may be seen as producing a work that is best described as a research report; in many ways it stands apart from the main thrust of the Alexandrian mathematical tradition, even the Greek tradition as a whole. Apollonius's *Conics* contains both textbook and research elements. The earlier and better-preserved portion is the more elementary—less concerned with the more difficult research aspects.

There is a pattern behind this. The works that survived from the late Greek era are all too often those works that were well regarded as textbooks. More advanced material, even from earlier ages, was often neglected. Thus, Euclid's *Elements* survives, but his *Conics* does not. Even if this latter was seen as having been rendered obsolete by the later work of Apollonius, that work, too, survives only in part.

Thus Hypatia, as she continued and extended her father's program of editing, commenting on, preserving, and teaching from the Alexandrian mathematical classics, was pushing that program into new and less charted waters.

What little we can reconstruct, however, of her endeavors in this direction tends to incline us to the view that her contributions consisted of a careful dotting of the *i*'s and a systematic crossing of the *t*'s in these more challenging and difficult works. Doubtless this was done to meet the perceived needs of weak and struggling students, but it makes for work that was probably adjudged difficult and of limited interest both in its own time and in the ensuing years, and it also makes for work of limited interest to us, but for a different reason: because it has very limited mathematical content. It can be a useful didactic exercise, for example, to check that the "answers" to algebraic problems actually do work, and one can imagine Hypatia's students benefiting from such drill. It makes, however, very dull reading for later historians, whose interests are, naturally enough, different.

By the 390s, Hypatia was teaching mathematics and philosophy in Alexandria, and if we consider that Synesius learned from her and, as far as we can ascertain, from no one else, then Hypatia was Alexandria's preeminent mathematician at that time. Furthermore, we have it on Synesius's authority that there was little of intellectual interest in the Athens of that day. It was to be some years before Proclus left Alexandria and helped to revive the Athenian school. There was little other mathematical activity elsewhere in the Roman Empire. It was rather a low point.

So it is quite clear, if we accept that Theon likely predeceased his daughter, that at the relevant time Hypatia was the empire's most accomplished mathematician. This also implies that she, like her father, was very likely the leading mathematician in the world. It was not a good time for mathematics in either China or in India. The achievements of the Arabs lay well in the future. If there is to be any other claimant for the top position in the late fourth and early fifth centuries of our era, probably that claimant would have to be Persian, but no name has been adduced.

It may come as a disappointment to some to learn that although Hypatia was in her time the world's best mathematician, she cannot realistically be classed as one of the world's great mathematicians. However, if one considers that the times were not at all conducive to mathematical research, that the institutions that had supported such work were gone, and that mathematicians themselves were under great suspicion, then this should not really surprise us.

Indeed, it is misguided if understandable feminism to exaggerate Hypatia's importance in the history of mathematics merely because she was a woman. One should not make her out to be something she was not; rather, one should look at what her achievements actually were. Once we forget the impulse to aggrandize her accomplishments in line with our own preconceptions, we open the way to recognize her very considerable real achievements.

In the first place, she is to be regarded as a teacher—a charismatic and versatile teacher. Her lectures were popular, her pupils loyal and admiring. Although a pagan in a predominantly Christian environment, her followers came from both camps and may have included Jews as well.

Another point that could be made is that, on the account I have given, for Hypatia, mathematics was not studied merely for its own sake. Rather it had a "sacred" significance, as a route to the One. It pointed to something beyond itself—indeed, beyond the power of human knowledge. This may perhaps be compared with our own present preoccupation with the practical uses of mathematics. The complicated mathematics involved in, for example, weather prediction does not exist for its own sake either, although of course the motivation that leads us to study *that* is extremely different.

Furthermore, the breadth of her interests is most impressive. Within mathematics, she wrote or lectured on astronomy (including its observational aspects—the astrolabe), geometry (and for its day advanced geometry at that), and algebra (again, for its time, difficult algebra), and made an advance in computational technique—all this as well as engaging in religious philosophy and aspiring to a good writing style.

Her writings were, as best we can judge, an outgrowth of her teaching in the technical areas of mathematics. In effect she was continuing a program initiated by her father: a conscious effort to preserve and to elucidate the great mathematical works of the Alexandrian heritage. These were to be adapted to the needs of pupils, and the style of presentation (insofar as we can glimpse it) was chosen for its didactic effectiveness. In her intellectual priorities within mathematics, she was thus very much her father's daughter.

It would seem that as a teacher she surpassed her father, because we have several independent testimonies to her eminence in this area, while no similar endorsement of Theon has come down to us. Theon seems to have been the better regarded, however, as a textbook writer. His editions and commentaries were much more carefully preserved by subsequent generations, perhaps because they treated more straightforward material, perhaps because they took as their originals more popular classic texts, or perhaps because they better met the needs of the era's students.

Beyond mathematics proper, we find an interest in science and some ability in this direction. The "hydroscope" is essentially a scientific instrument, with (it is true) a mathematical basis for its operation, but one not related directly to the other branches of mathematics that she professed. Her presumed interest in Synesius's theory of dreams may be taken to be yet another example of a scientific bent.

Again, there is the interest in philosophy proper, which impressed

PLATE 1. An armillary sphere, the instrument described in chapter 9, section G, and appendix A, section D. This example was built by Brian Greig of Southern Skies Astronomy Centre, Melbourne, Australia, and is in the possession of the author. The photograph is by Steve Morton, Department of Physics, Monash University.

PLATE 2. The front of a small astrolabe (diameter about 10 cm), the instrument described in chapter 9, section G, and appendix A, section D. The baseplate, with its sets of engraved lines at the very back, is the *mater*. Forward of this and able to rotate with respect to it is an elaborate and ornate netlike structure (the *rete*) incorporating most prominently the ecliptic circle marked with the various signs of the zodiac. The prominent linear structure running from top left to bottom right is the *rule* (a subsidiary structure to aid in the reading of the instrument), and forward of this is a locking pin (running from lower left to upper right).

It belongs to Robin G. Turner, formerly of the Department of Physics, Monash University. *(Photograph by Steve Morton)*

PLATE 3. The back of the instrument depicted in plate 2. Its prominent features are a representation of the ecliptic (with the signs of the zodiac) around the rim and the *alidade* (the linear structure running from top left to bottom right). Just visible are the sight-holes in this that enable the elevations of stars to be measured. For this purpose the instrument was suspended by the ring at the top, thus ensuring that it was aligned vertically. *(Photograph by Steve Morton)*

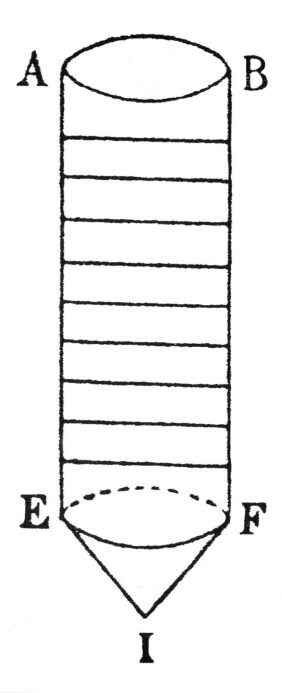

PLATE 4. A diagrammatic representation of Synesius's "Hydroscope," that is, hydrometer. See chapter 9, section H, and appendix D, section D.2. The diagram is taken from the published minute of Fermat's discussion (*Œuvres de Fermat*, vol. 1, ed. P. Tannery and C. Henry [Paris: Gauthier-Villars, 1891], 362–65). In Synesius's terminology, ABFE is the "tube" and IFE the "baryllium." The horizontal lines represent the "notches."

Damascius and commanded the devotion of Synesius. The latter's *Dion* was in effect refereed by his teacher. She seems indeed to have had an eclectic mind.

All in all we have a picture of a dedicated teacher, a versatile one whose interests embraced virtually the whole of the mathematics of the time and extended beyond this to speculative philosophy and to scientific endeavor. We see in her life little of the compartmentalization of knowledge that such a recitation of achievement imposes upon modern ears. Rather, geometry was a route to the One, just as was a celibate lifestyle. Arithmetic and even astronomy were similarly sacred. We may well imagine that the conservation and transmission of knowledge was a matter of passionate concern for her.

It was a response to difficult times, a brave response, an intellectual response, indeed a mathematical response.

And yes, we would like to know more of her. So much is lost and is now quite irrecoverable. But the main outlines of her life and her accomplishment are clear and they command our admiration.

# Appendix A

# MATHEMATICAL DETAILS

## A. NUMBER REPRESENTATION AND LONG DIVISION

*T*he standard Greek alphabet contains twenty-four letters, but an earlier version of it had twenty-seven. These twenty-seven letters were the basis of the Greek method of representing numbers. The first nine of the letters were taken to stand for the numbers 1–9, the next nine for the numbers 10–90, and the final nine for the numbers 100–900. Thus, any number from 1 to 999 could be simply and unambiguously represented. For instance, the letter $\tau$ stood for 300, $\kappa$ for 20, and $\beta$ for 2; thus, $\tau\kappa\beta$ represented the number 322.

With numbers larger than 999, a variety of devices were pressed into service. For Theon and Hypatia, the method was to combine the Greek literal notation with the Babylonian base-60 representation. In theory this meant that only the numbers 1 through 59 were required in the Greek, the rest being dealt with by means of a place notation not unlike our own. Thus 322 could be represented as $(5 \times 60) + 22$ and written $\varepsilon\ \kappa\beta$ (the $\varepsilon$ standing for 5). In practice, however, the two systems were combined, and this simplification was not always routinely used. The Babylonian system was always employed when it came to fractions.

For the remainder of this discussion, I will use our own familiar numerical symbols in place of the Greek, as nothing of real importance is lost thereby.

The Greek value for the number of days in the year was 365 14 48, which we are to understand as being 365 + (14/60) + (48/3,600). In our notation this is 365.24666. . . . (We may compare this with the currently accepted value of 365.242199 days.) The long division calculation that Hypatia performed in Book III of the Commentary on the *Almagest* was to determine the number of degrees of arc swept out in consequence in a single day, that is to say, 360/365.24666 . . . (on her figure).

The first part of the calculation involved dividing 365 14 48 by 60. This is easy as it involves little more than a shift in place value (as when *we* divide by ten). The result is seen to be

$$6\ 5\ 14\ 48, \text{ as } 365 = 6 \times 60 + 5.$$

Progressively add this number first to itself, then to the result of each previous calculation, and so construct a table. We find (in abridged form) the table below.

| | | | | |
|---|---|---|---|---|
| 1 | 6 | 5 | 14 | 48 |
| 2 | 12 | 10 | 29 | 36 |
| 3 | 18 | 15 | 44 | 24 |
| 4 | 24 | 20 | 59 | 12 |
| 5 | 30 | 26 | 14 | 0 |
| 6 | 36 | 31 | 28 | 48 |
| 7 | 42 | 36 | 43 | 36 |
| 8 | 48 | 41 | 58 | 24 |
| 9 | 54 | 47 | 13 | 12 |
| 10 | 60 | 52 | 28 | 0 |
| 20 | 121 | 44 | 56 | 0 |
| 30 | 182 | 37 | 24 | 0 |
| 40 | 243 | 29 | 52 | 0 |
| 50 | 304 | 22 | 20 | 0 |
| 60 | 365 | 14 | 48 | 0 |

We may now use this table to perform the division. From the entries for 50 and for 9, we discover that

$$59 \times (6\ 5\ 14\ 48) = 359\ 9\ 33\ 12,$$

just a little short of 360. In fact, the deficit is 0 50 26 48. We may think of this as 50 26 48, for the place value will automatically take care of the slight change involved. We note that the entry

$$8 \times (6\ 5\ 14\ 48) = 48\ 41\ 58\ 24$$

will leave the smallest positive remainder. The deficit now is

$$(50\ 26\ 48\ 0) - (48\ 41\ 58\ 24),$$

that is to say,

$$1\ 44\ 49\ 36, \text{ or } 104\ 49\ 36.$$

Again we search the table for the multiplier that gives the best under-estimate of this figure. The relevant entry is that for 17. We now calculate the product

$$17 \times (6\ 5\ 14\ 48) = (103\ 29\ 11\ 36),$$

and this time the deficit is

$$1\ 20\ 24\ 24, \text{ or } 80\ 24\ 24.$$

We may continue to proceed in this manner to discover the sequence of numbers 59, 8, 17 (already found), 13, 12, 31. Thus the quotient is the number 59 8 17 13 12 31, which in our notation is 0.985635278, the correct answer, or almost so. There is a slight discrepancy of procedure on the very last step in that the final figure, 31, is the closest approximation available rather than the closest underestimate.

A similar computation in Book IV is performed along similar lines. In Book I, by contrast, a long division is performed for illustrative purposes. The actual computation is

$$(1515\ 20\ 15) \div (25\ 12\ 10)$$

and by means of a less expeditious trial-and-error method the approximation 60 7 33 is produced. The computation in Book IX follows the tabular method in part. It is marred, however, by frequent misprints and its expository style is different.

## B. CONIC SECTIONS

The standard approach today to the study of the conic sections is to consider the various possibilities when a so-called right circular cone is intersected by a plane. We may without loss of generality take the right circular cone to consist of all the lines joining a given circle to a point on its axis (the line through its center and perpendicular to the plane of the circle itself). To fix ideas, let the circle be that described by the equations $x^2 + y^2 = a^2$; $z = 0$. The axis is now the $z$-axis, $x = y = 0$, and without loss of generality we may take the point to be $P = (0, 0, 1)$.

By symmetry, it is possible to restrict the possible planes of section and yet retain full generality. It is enough to consider the cone to be cut by the plane $z = kx$, for any positive constant $k$. If

$$k < \frac{1}{a}$$

we generate the curve known as the *ellipse*, that is, a perspective rendering of a circle (and indeed, the special case $k = 0$ yields a circle, the original circle); if

$$k = \frac{1}{a}$$

the curve is a *parabola*; and if

$$k > \frac{1}{a}$$

the curve is known as a *hyperbola*. In the limit as $k$ approaches $\infty$, the hyperbola approximates a pair of intersecting straight lines.

This simple approach was, however, not that of Apollonius. He took instead a *scalene*, or *oblique*, cone. In this case the point $P$ was not necessarily on the axis, but (in modern terms) at (again with appropriate choice of coordinates, and without loss of generality) $(c, 0, 1)$. We get, in the event that we intersect this cone with the plane $x = 0$, an ellipse if $c > a$, a parabola if $c = a$, and a hyperbola if $c < a$. The parabola is the special case referred to in chapter 9, section D. The other two are the more general ones discussed in detail by Knorr.

It may perhaps be worth mentioning that Apollonius's oblique cone is in fact the same as a right elliptical cone. We may get the same figures if we replace the circle

$$x^2 + y^2 = a^2$$

by an ellipse

$$b^2x^2 + a^2y^2 = a^2b^2$$

and keep $P$ as $(0, 0, 1)$. It would at first sight appear that this was a more general situation than that of modern treatments, but this is not so. It merely "stretches" the conic so generated. Such stretching (equivalent to a perspective drawing of the original curve) leaves ellipses as ellipses, hyperbolas as hyperbolas, and parabolas as parabolas. We thus have a major economy in the modern approach, and mathematically this is an advantage. To understand the history, however, we must look at things from the earlier point of view.

## C. DIOPHANTINE ANALYSIS

Diophantus's *Arithmetic* poses a set of problems, classified in order of algebraic complexity and seeking the solutions to various equations posed in verbal form. The required solutions are to involve only rational numbers (i.e., exact ratios of whole numbers) and there is, in the main, less attempt at general (complete) solution, but rather the demonstration of various particular solutions. However, in many cases the particular solutions are reached by methods that easily generalize, so it is assumed that Diophantus saw his particular solutions as illustrations of more general results. A well-known example is given below.

His work is seen as important on two principal grounds. First, it takes the initial steps toward modern algebraic notation by introducing abbreviations into the verbal descriptions of the problem; second, the emphasis on rational solutions (in many instances equivalent to a search for integral, i.e., whole number, solutions) gave rise, in the hands of Euler, Fermat, and others, to the modern field of diophantine analysis.

A feel for what is involved may be gained from Problem 8 of Book II. This reads (in modern translation):

To divide a given square number into two squares.

Given square number 16.
$x^2$ one of the required squares. Therefore $16 - x^2$ must be equal to a square.
Take a square of the form $(mx - 4)^2$, $m$ being any integer and 4 the number which is the square root of 16, e.g., take
$(2x - 4)^2$, and equate it to $16 - x^2$.

Therefore $4x^2 - 16x + 16 = 16 - x^2$, or $5x^2 = 16x$, and $x = \dfrac{16}{5}$.

The required squares are therefore $\dfrac{256}{25}, \dfrac{144}{25}$.

We may note a number of features of this solution. First of all, it is a particular solution; the number 16 is quite explicit and later $m$ is specialized to 2. However, the *method* of attack is quite general. Indeed, many commentators feel that specific numbers like 16 are intended to be understood as illustrative representations of more general numbers. In this case, if the number 16 is replaced by the general $a$, then the result follows that

$$x = \frac{2ma}{m^2 + 1} \quad \text{and} \quad y \text{ (say)} = \sqrt{a^2 - x^2} = \frac{(m^2 - 1)a}{m^2 + 1}.$$

This is equivalent, modulo a few legal niceties, to a known general solution, usually presented in slightly different language by asking that $x$ and $y$ be, not merely rational numbers, but *integers*. The solution given by Diophantus is, of course, equivalent to an integral solution, namely,

$$16^2 + 12^2 = 20^2.$$

This is also the problem that led Fermat to claim the result, in a famous marginal note to his own copy of Diophantus, that the equation

$$x^n + y^n = a^n$$

had no solutions for any integers $x$, $y$, and $a$, for any positive integer $n$ greater than 2. This claim (one of the most famous statements in mathematics) is now known as Fermat's Last Theorem.

But note a complete change of emphasis here. Whereas Diophantus showed how particular equations might be solved, Fermat claimed a negative result: that an *entire class* of equation possesses *no* solution. Diophantus only rarely claimed a result of this kind. (Of course the equation $x^n + y^n = a^n$ does possess solutions if we drop the requirement that $x$, $y$, and $a$ be integral, and allow irrational values. This restriction has been one of Diophantus's major legacies to mathematics, although the modern version is not always the one he himself adopted.)

The two problems coming immediately before this famous and

influential one are much simpler. Problem 6 of Book II asks, in modern terms, for the solution of a pair of simultaneous equations

$$x - y = a; \ x^2 - y^2 = (x - y) + b \ ,$$

where $a$ and $b$ are known. The case solved is $a = 2$, $b = 20$. The rest is straightforward, and the reader may verify the answer $x = 13/2$, $y = 9/2$. Indeed, the general case is hardly more difficult. Problem 7, immediately following, is a trivial extension. The two problems present no points of mathematical interest.

These two problems are very probably interpolations, but it is not likely, in the light of recent discoveries of Arabic translations, that they are due to Hypatia, as was once thought. It would seem to be established that her contributions are to be found preserved in the Arabic text and the most likely place to look for them is in the detailed verification of the claimed solutions there given.

# D. STEREOGRAPHIC PROJECTION

The astrolabe could be used as a basic surveying device to find the angle between, say, the sun and zenith, or to determine the height of a mountain. But further, and more important, it enabled the determination of latitude and the direction of true north, even during the day when the stars were not visible. Beyond this, as long as the sun or some major star was visible, it enabled the determination of the time of day or night.

The celestial sphere, the apparent shape of the heavens with its fixed pattern of stars, may be analyzed exactly as a replica of the terrestrial globe. If we imagine the earth's axis to be infinitely prolonged so as to intersect the heavens, then these points of intersection will define the north and south celestial poles. The north celestial pole is very close to the so-called pole star (Polaris). Midway between the celestial poles is the circle of the celestial equator, and between the poles and the equator are circles of (celestial) latitude.

Because of the rotation of the earth, the celestial sphere will appear (to observers on the surface of the earth and thinking of themselves as fixed in space) to rotate once over the course of each twenty-four hours. This apparent rotation will take place about an axis that passes from the north to the south celestial pole. Each star, therefore, will trace out a circle in the observer's sky. This circle will be a circle of latitude on the celestial sphere.

This is one way of looking at the matter. Another is to take the sky as seen by the observer at any one time. Directly overhead is the point of zenith, and below this is a hemisphere of the celestial sphere: the visible part lying above the observer's horizon. Between these extremes are circles of what we might call "observer latitude": 80° above the horizon is an 80° circle, and so on. (The technical name for such a circle of "observer latitude" is an *almucantar*.) The observer's celestial sphere will be tilted with respect to the standard one and vice versa. For an observer at the North Pole, the two would coincide. Otherwise the tilt applies. Thus, for an observer at, say, 31° north latitude (the approximate latitude of Alexandria), the north celestial pole will be 31° above the horizon, or 59° below the zenith.

Equivalently, we may adopt a standard orientation and thus seek to accommodate the peculiar features of the observer's latitude. Take the observer's celestial sphere and so orient it that the north celestial pole is at the top (and the south celestial pole at the bottom). The geometry involved is shown in cross section in figure 1 on page 124. The north celestial pole will still be on the 31° circle above the observer's horizon (or 59° below the zenith). This circle is one of a number of almucantars that could be drawn on the now tilted observer's celestial sphere.

Passing through this tilted sphere is the plane of the celestial equator. Consider now the set of lines connecting the south celestial pole to one of these almucantars, say, the 31° circle that just touches the equator. Each of these lines will pass through the plane of the celestial equator, and together they define a curve upon it. This curve is in fact a circle. See figure 2 on page 125, which shows this 31° almucantar. Indeed, each of the almucantars gives rise to such a circle. We may make a diagram

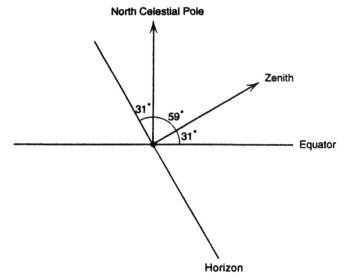

**Figure 1. A cross section of the "tilt" as applicable to Alexandria.** The celestial equator is shown as horizontal, and zenith is 31° above this. The observer's horizon is thus shown inclined. The observer's experience, of course, is that zenith is vertically above. To recover this point of view, rotate the diagram.

of the various circles set up by so projecting each of the almucantars onto the plane of the celestial equator. It is this pattern of circles that forms one of the sets of lines engraved on the mater and the climates of the astrolabe. The equator itself and also the tropics of Cancer and Capricorn also project as circles. The Tropic of Capricorn was usually taken as the rim of the instrument. Any almucantars that intersected this tropic therefore were shown only in part; others appeared in full.

(It should be noted that the above theory applies to an astrolabe designed for use in the *Northern Hemisphere*. The very few astrolabes intended for use in the *Southern Hemisphere* took their point of projection as the *north* celestial pole. Throughout this discussion, it is assumed that the Northern Hemisphere is the one in question.)

Similarly, lines of equal azimuth, which are lines of "observer longitude," as the almucantars are lines of "observer latitude," project by this same means into circles, and these, too, are engraved onto the mater and the various climates.

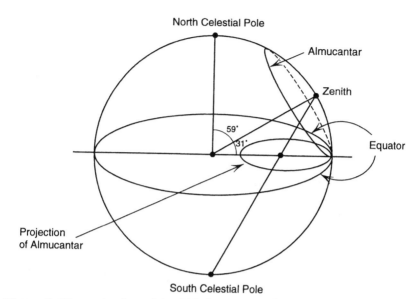

**Figure 2.** The projection of the 31° almucantar, shown in a perspective rendering. The lines through the south celestial pole and through the oblique circle (the 31° almucantar) intersect the plane of the equator in another circle. Each other almucantar does likewise (although the various circles so produced are not concentric). Almucantars closer to the zenith will project as circles lying within the equatorial circle; those farther away as circles that intersect the equatorial circle. The *mater* of the astrolabe reproduced these equatorial projections. Usually it terminated with the circle representing the Tropic of Capricorn; almucantars that intersected *that* circle thus appeared only in part, as circular arcs.

A third set of lines was engraved on the mater of the instrument as well. These were curves representing the various "hour angles"; the details of these will here be omitted.

The rete was designed to represent the various major stars: most notably those of the constellations of the zodiac. These are those parts of the sky through which the sun appears to pass in the course of a year, as ascertained by its points of rising and setting. These lie about another circle in the celestial sphere known as the *ecliptic*. The ecliptic also projects into a circle and this was molded in metal to form the principal feature of the rete. The positions of the various stars occupy fixed positions with respect to the ecliptic. The rete was a highly intricate patterned device, whose shape incorporated the circular arc of the ecliptic and various points that represented the major fixed stars.

Thus, the rete gives the fixed positions of the fixed stars in their positions in the celestial sphere, and does so in a two-dimensional format. This remains unchanged whatever the position of the observer. The mater (and the climates), by contrast, show those features of the situation that depend upon the position (i.e., the latitude) of the observer. Thus in applications to navigation, one rete suffices (as long as the various stars used in it remain visible), but the appropriate climate must be inserted to replace the mater.

The third, and simplest, component is the alidade. This is essentially a sighting device. By aligning the line of sight to some major star along the alidade, and reading off the angle from a scale engraved on the back of the mater, the star's angle of elevation could be determined.

From simple observations of this type and by the use of rotations of the rete relative to the mater (or the appropriate climate), as well as by use of the various tables that might be engraved on the back of the mater, the astrolabe enabled the mechanical, or partly mechanical, computation of time, direction, and other such quantities. It was known to (probably) Hipparchus, a pre-Ptolemaic astronomer born around 180 BCE, and continued in use till the seventeenth century CE.

Each of the computations depended on the correct placement of some point of the rete relative to the relevant climate, and this in turn duplicated the corresponding operation on an armillary sphere. The portability of the instrument, its small size (typically some 25 cm across), and its ease of handling made it popular and practical.

The armillary sphere is, in essence, a scale model of the heavens, so that computations relating to the real-life situation may be carried out by means of simulations performed on the model. The theory of stereographic projection allows the use, instead of the sphere, of a less obvious replica, but one in which all the essential features are preserved and which has the advantages of portability and practicality.

# Appendix B

# PANDROSION

$\mathcal{U}$ntil recently, it was usually asserted that Hypatia was the first woman mathematician of whom we had reliable knowledge. This opinion now requires revision, although it is true that she remains the first of whom we have any reasonably detailed information.

However, we now have some sketchy but definite details of another earlier woman mathematician, also active in Alexandria, but some two generations before Hypatia. Her name was Pandrosion, and she was a contemporary of Pappus, indeed a rival, for Pappus speaks quite slightingly of her. Whether she had any influence on Hypatia is not known.

Previously, Pandrosion was supposed to be a man and was referred to as "Pandrosio." The change of viewpoint is the result of careful detective work by various scholars who discovered that the published text of Pappus's *Collection* contained a number of major errors. Among these was the alteration of Pandrosion's name and sex from the primary manuscript to the printed version. It is now abundantly clear that she was a woman.

We also know something of the mathematics she did. A geometric construction to produce (approximations to) cube roots is quite definitely associated with her—though whether she developed it herself or merely taught it is not at all clear.

Pappus described the method in some detail in Book III of his *Collection*, and did so with the avowed purpose of pouring scorn upon it.

This is in fact an unfair assessment, as the method works, more or less as well as the other techniques then available.

For the reader's convenience, I here reprint Winifred Frost's article "Pappus and the Pandrosion Puzzlement" from the Monash University journal of school mathematics, *Function*. This was an early discussion of the matter and for a general audience is still the best point of entry into a complex subject.

# PAPPUS AND THE PANDROSION PUZZLEMENT

*Winifred Frost*

Pappos of Alexandria (Pappus is the Latinized version) was a Greek mathematician of the 4th century AD, whose work comes some six centuries after Euclid, when the great geometrical tradition was kept alive by teachers like him who wrote commentaries on the works of their famous predecessors. He was mentioned by the later writers Marinus and Proclus at Athens in the 5th century and Eutocius at Alexandria in the 6th, as a commentator on Euclid and Ptolemy. There are also two later references to him; one placed him at the beginning of the 4th century, the other at the end of it. He is known to us as the author of "The Collection," which consists of eight books of which the first, half the second, and perhaps the end of the eighth are missing. Pandrosion is the person to whom he addressed the third book, and thereby hangs a tale.

Nothing would be known of the "Collection" if it were not for the survival of a single manuscript, now known as *Vaticanus Graecus 218*, which had reached the Vatican Library by the 16th century, and was probably copied in Byzantium in the 9th or 10th century. How many removes it is from Pappus's original manuscript cannot be known unless another earlier manuscript is found, but it may be only one or two, including that of the copyist who prepared the work for publication. It is disorganized, contains repetitions and mistakes, and could not have been prepared for publication by Pappus himself. Eleven other manuscripts of the remnants of it, mostly 16th century, exist, as well as several with only some or one of the books, but they have all been proved to be copied from the *Vaticanus* itself or its descendants.

Until the first printed edition of Federicus Commandinus was published posthumously in Pesaro, Italy, in 1588, very few had access to Pappus's work, but Commandinus extended its readership with a Latin translation, omitting the part of Book II. No other edition was printed until 1875, when Fridericus Hultsch's edition was published in Berlin, with Greek on the left page and Latin on the right. This is still the standard edition. The only edition in a modern language is the French translation of Hultsch's text by Paul Ver Eecke, published in 1933. These are the only complete texts available to a modern scholar, sixteen centuries after Pappus wrote.

Hultsch's edition was based largely on a secondary manuscript, *Paris 2440*, though he was aware that the *Vaticanus* was superior, and had been able to consult Books II to VI. He also consulted two other manuscripts, but the advantages of photography and modern means of travel were not available to him. So it is only quite recently that further progress has been made to make the "Collection" more accessible to those who have no Latin or Greek. (The outline of its contents may be found in "A Manual of Greek Mathematics" by Sir Thomas Heath, the famous 19th century translator of Euclid's "Elements," and of Archimedes, Apollonius, and Diophantus.)

Australia has its own Pappus scholar, Professor A. Treweek, former Professor of Greek at Sydney University. He obtained photocopies of the *Vaticanus* in 1938, and comparing Hultsch's text with it, "realized that all was not well with it." After the war he copied out the whole *Vaticanus* (a truly modern scribe!) which is difficult to read, as it is in a minuscule hand and some letters have quite different form from today's script. He spent study leaves in 1949–50 and 1955–56 collating all the other extant manuscripts, either by personal inspection or from photostats, noting all variations of the texts on the left-hand pages of his manuscript. He greatly contributed to the advance of the study of Pappus by restoring many illegible passages where water damage had occurred. He did this by deciphering the mirror image offset visible on the opposite page. In the course of his work, he proved from relationships between the manuscripts that they all stem from the *Vaticanus*, and that its date was 10th century, or possibly 9th. By reading what was visible after rebinding of numbers marking the beginning of a quaternion or quire (of four sheets folded once), he deduced that the missing quires must number either two or six. His doctoral thesis contained his transcription of Books II to VI and his report on the manuscripts and their relationships. The latter was published in the scholarly journal *Scriptorium* in 1957.

Further research continues to be done. In 1986, A. Jones's translation of Book VII was published. This is the most historically interesting book, listing the books that made up the "domain of analysis," works by Euclid, Apollonius, and Aristaeus (many of which we would otherwise know nothing about) and showing the method of proof of propositions by analysis of what must precede if the proposition is assumed to be true, until something given or known is reached, and then by synthesis, that is by the reverse process, or building up of the proof.

More recently a very scholarly work, "Textual Studies in Ancient and Medieval Geometry," by W. R. Knorr examines the texts, their contents, history, and relationships, of eight commentators on the works of the ancient mathematicians, from Heron of Alexandria in the first century, to Eutocius and John Philoponus in the sixth, and including Pappus, Theon, and Hypatia.

My interest in Pappus began when I was looking for a long-term project that would combine my interest in mathematics and classics, and Bob Berghout of Newcastle University told me that there was no English translation of the "Collection." In the way of fools who rush in, I began at once with Book II, which shows how to multiply any quantity of single letter numbers together by taking out all factors of ten, and multiplying only the base numbers together. Factors of ten are again taken out, their total number is divided by four, and the number of myriads (10000s) is obtained. He quotes Apollonius as his source.

Book III is more interesting. There are four unrelated sections containing 45 propositions and 15 lemmas. The first section is concerned with the ancient problem of the duplication of the cube (equivalent to finding two mean proportionals between two given quantities); the second shows how, in certain cases, a triangle may be constructed on the base of, and inside another triangle, yet have its other two sides together greater than, equal to, or in given ratio to the remaining sides of the outer triangle, and extends to polygons with four or more sides. The third section shows how ten different means between two given quantities may be obtained, and how, given an extreme quantity and the mean, to find the other extreme quantity; the fourth shows how to inscribe in a given sphere the five regular polyhedra—pyramid, cube, octahedron, dodecahedron, and icosahedron. His method differs from Euclid's in Book 13 of the *Elements*, and is probably based on Theodosius's *Spherics*.

At the very beginning of Book III one gets a taste of Pappus's style. He addresses it to Pandrosion ("dedicates" is not the right word), only to show his low opinion of her students. "Certain people," he says, "who claim to have learned mathematics from you, set out the enunciation of the problems in what seemed to us an ignorant manner." In his account of the duplication of the cube, he gives no credit to the unknown student ("an important person, reputed to be a geometer"), though he does not recognize that his method of approximating the two means [the cube root and its square] is at least as good as the other ancient methods, which of course were sanctified by age. In fact it is an iterative procedure, obtaining successive improving approximations, and it may be proved by modern methods that the approximations converge to the exact solution. Again in the propositions on finding the means, he scorns the effort of "a certain other person" to exhibit the arithmetic, geometric, and harmonic means on a semi-circle, which he does using only four lines, and says: "but how BZ is a mean of the harmonic mediety, or of which straight lines, he does not say," even though it is not difficult to prove that it is, and of the same two lines as for the other two means. So we begin to see a conceited irascible old gent, fallible himself, but intolerant of the faults of others. (Perhaps his name, Pappos—grandfather, is indicative of something other than reverence?) There are several other examples in Books VI and VII of his critical attitude to other scholars.

One wonders whether his criticism would have been quite so terse if Pandrosion had not been a woman. Yet she certainly was; all the manuscripts have the feminine vocative form of the adjective translated as "most excellent," which Hultsch has changed from the long *e* (eta), to the short *e* (epsilon), of the masculine vocative case. Emendations should never be undertaken without careful thought, and there are clues in the name itself to warn against it. The *-ion* ending is a diminutive or pet name ending, as we say Jimmy for James, and the original, Pandrosos, was the name of one of three sister-goddesses, daughters of Cecrops and Aglauros in Greek myth. It means "all dewy," not a likely male epithet. Following Hultsch, Ver Eecke calls her Pandrosio, using the modern male termination. Three other books have dedications: Books VII and VIII to "my son Hermodorus" (no doubt of his sex, though he may not actually have been Pappus's son), and Book V to Megithion, otherwise unknown, but all the manuscripts have the masculine adjective.

So we have in Pandrosion a female teacher of mathematics at Alexandria, probably a younger contemporary of Pappus, perhaps even at the same institution, the Museum (or University). Pappus's date was determined in the 1930s by A. Rome from his observation of an eclipse of the sun in 320 AD, mentioned in his commentary on Ptolemy's "Almagest," part of which survives, and since he therefore pre-dates Theon, father of Hypatia, there is at least one, and perhaps two generations between Pandrosion and Hypatia. This means that it is Pandrosion and not Hypatia for whom we may make the claim "first known woman mathematician." And perhaps more may have been heard of her, if she, like Hypatia, had been the daughter of a famous mathematician.

Since completing the translation of Book III, Bob Berghout and I have visited Professor Treweek at his home. He is now [1992] eighty, and was so pleased that two more Australians were taking up his *"vitai lampada"* that he has given us his precious manuscript copy of the *Vaticanus*, his volumes of Hultsch's and Ver Eecke's translations, the *Scriptorium* article, and other valuable books, for which no thanks would be adequate. Our aim is to continue with the work of a complete English text and commentary, of which the mathematical and historical aspect is Bob Berghout's field, while I translate and revise with his invaluable help.

# *Appendix C*
# THE LEGEND OF SAINT CATHERINE OF ALEXANDRIA

For approximately a thousand years, Saint Catherine of Alexandria was one of the most venerated saints in the entire Christian calendar. Among the many artists who depicted her were Caravaggio, Correggio, Cranach, Dürer, Murillo, Raphael, Rubens, Titian, and Tintoretto. She was listed as one of fourteen especially saintly women: the fourteen "holy helpers," and was named as the patron saint of some thirty groups of people. Yet it is highly doubtful that she ever existed!

The two sources for her "life" are a *Conversio* and a *Passio*, both without any real historical basis.

The first of these tells of her royal birth, her wondrous beauty, her learning, and her subsequent conversion to Christianity. It relates that shortly after her baptism she contracted a "mystic marriage" with Christ, who appeared to her in the course of a vision. That is to say, she embraced a life of dedicated virginity. Her name, in fact, is a reflection of this; it is derived from the Greek *Aeikatharina*, which means "the woman ever pure."

The *Passio* continues her story by recounting that fifty pagan philosophers sent to persuade her to return to paganism were instead converted to the Christian faith by her eloquence and learning; that she further persuaded the empress to profess Christianity, herself refused the advances of the emperor Maxentius, and that these acts led to her martyrdom. She was set upon a spiked wheel and tortured, but the wheel broke and the spikes (or perhaps razors) flew off to cut the throats of the onlookers. She was subsequently decapitated, which succeeded in killing her even though milk rather than blood flowed from the wound in her neck. The account ends with angels transporting her body to Mount Sinai, where alleged relics are still venerated by monks of the Eastern Church.

Her cult began in the eighth century when her body was supposedly "discovered" and a monastery was built to house her remains and to foster her veneration. By the tenth century, devotion to her was both very well established and also widespread. She was established as the patron of, inter alia, maidens, nurses (from the milk she bled), wheelwrights, millers, spinners, philosophers, teachers, jurists, and the clergy. One of her fingers is supposed to have reached Magdeburg in the late Middle Ages. In art she is depicted with a book, a quill pen (knowledge in both cases), a ring (mystic marriage), a crown (royal birth), a wheel, or a sword (decapitation). However, because of the lack of any real evidence that she ever existed, she became something of an embarrassment and the Roman Church suppressed her cult in 1969.

We have briefly noted, in chapter 5, an attempt to arrogate Hypatia to the Christian cause, and there are enough elements common to the Catherine legend and Hypatia's story to suggest that something of the same has happened here. We have the wondrous beauty, the learning, the standing among philosophers, the dedicated virginity, the wheel (Hypatia was dragged down from her chariot), and the martyrdom. The inconvenient fact that Hypatia was killed *by* Christians, a martyr to her pagan faith, is thus quietly overlooked. The other aspects of the Catherine legend are explicable enough as the not uncommon hyperbole of hagiography.

# TRANSLATIONS OF THE PRIMARY SOURCES

## A. THE *SUDA*, HESYCHIUS, AND DAMASCIUS

### 1. The Suda entry on Hypatia

**HYPATIA**

The daughter of Theon the geometer, a philosopher of Alexandria, and herself a philosopher and well known to many people. Wife of the philosopher Isidorus. Flourished in the time of the emperor Arcadius. She wrote a commentary on Diophantus, [one on] the Canon of Astronomy, and a commentary on the Conics of Apollonius. She was torn to pieces by the Alexandrians, and her body was mutilated, and scattered through all the city. This she suffered because of spite for her outstanding wisdom especially in matters of astronomy; according to some at the hands of Cyril, to others because of the innate unruliness and rebelliousness of the Alexandrians. For they also did this to many of the bishops among them; look at Georgius and Proterion.

*About Hypatia the philosopher; proof of the factiousness of the Alexandrians.*

She was born, raised, and educated in Alexandria. In nature more noble than her father, she was not satisfied with her education in mathematics by her father but also gained knowledge of philosophy the other not ignoble [study]. Donning the robe of a scholar, the lady made appearances around the center of the city, expounding in public to those willing to listen on Plato or Aristotle or any other philosopher.

In teaching also she achieved the peak of excellence, and though naturally modest and fair-minded, she remained unwed, and she was so exceedingly beautiful and fair of form that one of her colleagues fell in love with her. And he could not control his passion, but made his affections obvious to her. Some uninformed stories say that Hypatia cured him of his sickness with music, but the truth long ago reported that tales of music were nonsense, and that bringing out one of her feminine napkins she thrust [or threw] it at him; and having displayed the evidence of her unclean nature said: "It is this you love, young man, not beauty"; and he, put off by shame and horror at this unseemly display, disposed his heart more temperately.

This was Hypatia's style: in speech articulate and logical, in her actions prudent and public-spirited, and the rest of the city gave her suitable welcome and accorded her special respect. The archons handling the affairs of the city would always go to see her first, as continued to happen also at Athens. For if the practice of philosophy had declined, still its reputation was seen to be revered and respected by those managing the most important affairs of the state.

Now once it happened that Cyril, who was bishop of the opposing religious sect, was passing Hypatia's house, and saw that there was a great crush around the doors, "a confusion of men and horses," of people coming and going, and others standing about. And when he asked what the crowd was, and why there was a commotion at the house, he heard from his attendants that Hypatia the philosopher was now going to address them, and that this was her house. When he learned this, he was so outraged that he swiftly plotted her death, the most unholy of all deaths. When she came forward as usual, a large mob of brutal men, so truly wicked, "aware neither of the retribution of the gods nor the revenge of men," laid hold of the philosopher and slew her, bringing on their land this most extreme shame and disgrace. The emperor would have been angered about this if [Anthemius] had not been bribed. And he took the price for her injuries and assumed them upon himself and his house and his children, and his descendant paid the penalty.

The memory of this event still preserved among the Alexandrians focussed the honor and esteem of the Alexandrians for Isidorus; with such fear hanging over them yet everyone was eager to be often in his company and listen to the words of moderation from his lips. And since so many of the rhetoricians were in charge of discussions or poetic studies they welcomed the large circle of the philosopher. For even if he was not expert in such things, he had something to add to the other (woman) philosopher in preciseness, and to them something more thorough in their own techniques. In other areas he was intensively questioned and on the speeches and poems offered would give a decision which differed from the others. Hence in the lecture rooms at a lecture in logic he had little praise for those giving a demonstration and his praise was quite restrained; yet it was appropriate and in accordance with the rules.

Thus practically the whole lecture room had the help of his criticism as a means of assessing those speaking as better or worse. Of those in my time I know three men of discernment able to judge things spoken without meter. For the same person it is agreed may be a critic of poetry and prose. I consider that the same person would be a craftsman in both; only if practice in each were equal and with equal keenness. I do not say that Isidorus was one of these; he did not nearly come up to the three. And the critics were Agapius, Severianus, and Nomus. Nomus was our contemporary.

## 2. Hesychius's Onomatologus

## HYPATIA

The daughter of Theon the geometer, a philosopher of Alexandria, and herself a philosopher and well known to many people. Wife of the philosopher Isidorus. Flourished in the time of the emperor Arcadius. She wrote a commentary on Diophantus, the Canon of Astronomy, and a commentary on the Conics of Apollonius. [She was torn to pieces by the Alexandrians, and her body was mutilated, and scattered through all the city. This she suffered because of spite for her outstanding wisdom especially in matters of astronomy; according to some at the hands of Cyril, to others because of the innate unruliness and rebelliousness of the Alexandrians. For they also did this to many of the bishops among them; look at Georgius and Proterion.]

## 3. Damascius's Life of Isidorus (first excerpt)

Epiphanius and Euprepius both came from Alexandria and were adepts in the cultic rituals of the Alexandrians. The so-called Persian mysteries were conducted by Euprepius, those of Osiris by Epiphanius; and not these alone but also those of the god worshipped as Aion. (What sort of a god this was I could in fact now say, but I do not at present wish to reveal.) So Epiphanius also celebrated the worship of this god. These men, moreover, no longer lived under the old dispensation, but clearly already belonged to the generation following immediately upon it, although they still retained contact with the former. Urged by these therefore, they showed their contemporaries the path to great blessings, by proclaiming with great fanfare, inter alia, the stories people tell of the past.

People told a story, characteristic of life in Alexandria, both religious and secular. . . .

[*The heroine of this story was Hypatia.*]

This woman was born, raised and educated in Alexandria. Moreover, since she was by nature of a more noble disposition than her father, she was not content with the mathematical education she was able to receive from her father's hand. She was further led by her noble enthusiasm into the other branches of philosophy. Though a woman, she assumed the scholar's mantle and made excursions through the center of the city. She explained, by public demand and to those willing to listen, Plato or Aristotle or any other philosopher. Furthermore and apart from her teaching skill she attained to eminence in the practice of virtue. She was honest and chaste and throughout her life remained a virgin. And yet she was very beautiful and well-proportioned.

As a result, even one of her pupils fell in love with her. Nor was he able to control his feelings, but on the contrary allowed even her to notice his passion. Although nowadays, uninformed reports relate that it was by means of music that Hypatia cured his illness, the real truth is otherwise. For musical knowledge (of this kind) had by then already long since been lost. But rather, producing a *bloodstained* menstrual napkin, she pointed to this evidence of the unclean nature of procreation and said, "In truth, this is the focus of your yearning, young man, but it is nothing beautiful!"

The Alexandrians referred to the napkins used in female hygiene as *phylakeia* (shieldcloths). . . .

[*These shield-cloths had earlier also played a role in the preservation of virginity. They had besides a related use in the marriage ceremony:*]

For the wedding was not valid unless the priests of the goddess had personally signed the marriage certificate. . . .

So he (the young man), seized with shame and horror at the unseemly display, was brought to a change of heart and a return to chastity. . . .

Hypatia's style was like this: she was not only well-versed in rhetoric and in dialectic, but she was as well wise in practical affairs and motivated by civic-mindedness. Thus she came to be widely and deeply trusted throughout the city, accorded welcome and addressed with honor. Furthermore, when an archon was elected to office, his first call was to her, just as was also the practice in Athens. So although nowadays those charged with the governance of the city have abandoned the practical application of philosophy, back then its name still had a great and wonderful cachet. Now the following event took place.

Cyril, the bishop of the [. . . ] opposite sect, was passing Hypatia's house and noticed a hubbub at the door, "a confusion of horses and of men," some coming, others going, and yet others standing and waiting. He asked what was the meaning of the gathering and why there was a commotion at the house. Then he heard from his attendants that they were there to greet the philosopher Hypatia and that this house was hers. This information gave his heart such a prick that he at once plotted her murder, the most unholy of all murders. So next time when, following her usual custom, she appeared on the street, a mob of brutal men at once rushed at her—truly wicked men "fearing neither the revenge of the gods nor the judgment of men"—and killed the philosopher. . . .

And while she was still feebly twitching, they beat her eyes out. . . .

As a result they laid upon the city the heaviest blood-guilt and the greatest disgrace and the emperor would have been angry about it [. . . *and would surely have punished the perpetrators severely. . .* ] had not Aidesius been bribed. He thus to be sure allowed the murder to go unpunished, but in doing so assumed the guilt upon himself and on his descendants to come and his descendant had to pay the price. . . .

## 4. Damascius's Life of Isidorus (second excerpt)

[*Isidorus followed in Hypatia's footsteps even though she met such a dreadful fate.*]

The memory of this event was still preserved among the Alexandrians; however it only marginally affected their esteem for Isidorus and their regard for him. Despite the very real fear hanging over them, they nonetheless continued, everyone in frequent contact with him and, whenever they had the chance, listening to the words of wisdom that issued from his mouth. . . .

| [*Suda*] | [*Photius*] |
|---|---|
| Besides, all the masters in the schools of rhetoric and of poetry welcomed their frequent meetings with the philosopher. . . . | Besides, when they themselves were uncertain on some question they would at once go to him as a friend will go to a friend. . . . |

[*Thus Isidorus ended up winning for himself a popular respect as great as, nay even greater than, that for Hypatia.*]

There was a very great difference between Isidorus and Hypatia, not simply insofar as she was merely a woman while he was a man, but also insofar as she was expert mainly in geometry while he was a true philosopher.

# B. SOCRATES SCHOLASTICUS

## 1. The Ecclesiastical History, *Book VII, Chapter XIII*

*Conflict between the Christians and Jews at Alexandria: and breach between the Bishop Cyril and the Prefect Orestes.*

About this time it happened that the Jewish inhabitants were driven out of Alexandria by Cyril the bishop on the following account. The Alexandrian public is more delighted with tumult than any other people: and if at any time it should find a pretext, breaks forth into the most intolerable excesses; for it never ceases from its turbulence without bloodshed. It happened on the present occasion that a disturbance arose among the populace, not from a cause of serious importance, but out of an evil that has become very popular in almost all cities, viz. a fondness for dancing exhibitions. In consequence of the Jews being disengaged from business on the Sabbath, and spending their time, not in hearing the Law, but in theatrical amusements, dancers usually collect great crowds on that day, and disorder is almost invariably produced. And although this was in some degree controlled by the governor of Alexandria, nevertheless the Jews continued opposing these measures. And although they are always hostile towards the Christians they were roused to still greater opposition against them on account of the dancers. When therefore Orestes the prefect was publishing an edict—for so they are accustomed to call public notices—in the theater for the regulation of the shows, some of Cyril's party were present to learn the nature of the orders about to be issued. There was among them a certain Hierax, a teacher of the rudimental branches of literature, and one who was a very enthusiastic listener of the bishop Cyril's sermons, and made himself conspicuous by his forwardness in applauding. When the Jews observed this person in the theatre, they immediately cried out that he had come there for no other purpose than to incite sedition among the people. Now Orestes had long regarded with jealousy the growing power of the bishops, because they encroached on the jurisdiction of the authorities appointed by the emperor, especially as Cyril wished to set spies over his proceedings; he therefore ordered Hierax to be seized, and publicly subjected him to the torture in the theatre. Cyril, on being informed of this, sent for the principal Jews, and threatened them with the utmost severities unless they desisted from their molestation of the Christians. The Jewish populace on hearing these menaces, instead of suppressing their violence, only became more furious, and were led to form conspiracies for the destruction of the Christians; one of these was of so desperate a character as to cause their entire expulsion from Alexandria; this I shall now describe. Having agreed that each of them should wear a ring on his finger made of the bark of a palm branch, for the sake of mutual recognition, they determined to make a nightly attack on the Christians. They therefore sent persons into the streets to raise an outcry that the church named after Alexander was on fire. Thus many Christians on hearing this ran out, some from one direction and some from another, in great anxiety to save their church. The Jews immediately fell upon and slew them; readily distinguishing each other by their rings. At daybreak the authors of this atrocity could not be concealed: and Cyril, accompanied by an immense crowd of people, going to their synagogues—for they so call their house of prayer—took them away from them, and drove the Jews out of the city, permitting the multitude to plunder their goods. Thus the Jews who had inhabited the city from the time of Alexander the Macedonian were expelled from it, stripped of all they possessed, and dispersed some in one direction and some in another. [One of them, a physician named Adamantus, fled to Atticus bishop of Constantinople, and professing Christianity, some time afterwards returned to Alexandria and fixed his residence there.] But Orestes the governor of Alexandria was filled with great indignation at these transactions, and was excessively grieved that a city of such magnitude should have been suddenly bereft of so large a portion of its population; he therefore at once communicated the whole affair to the emperor. Cyril also wrote to him, describing the outrageous conduct of the Jews; and in the meanwhile sent persons to Orestes who should mediate concerning a reconciliation: for this the people had urged him to do. And when Orestes refused to listen to friendly advances, Cyril extended toward him the book of gospels, believing that respect for religion would induce him to lay aside his resentment. When, however, even this had no pacific effect on the prefect, but he persisted in implacable hostility against the bishop, the following event afterwards occurred.

## 2. Ibid., Chapter XIV

*The Monks of Nitria come down and raise a Sedition against the Prefect of Alexandria.*

Some of the monks inhabiting the mountains of Nitria, of a very fiery disposition, whom Theophilus some time before had unjustly armed against Dioscorus and his brethren, being again transported with an ardent zeal, resolved to fight in behalf of Cyril. About five hundred of them therefore quitting their monasteries, came into the city; and meeting the prefect in his chariot, they called him a pagan idolater, and applied to him many abusive epithets. He supposing this to be a snare laid for him by Cyril, exclaimed that he was a Christian, and had been baptized by Atticus the bishop at Constantinople. As they gave but little heed to his protestations, and a certain one of them named Ammonius threw a stone at Orestes which struck him in the head, and covered him with blood that flowed from the wound, all the guards with a few exceptions fled, plunging into the crowd, some in one direction and some in another, fearing to be stoned to death. Meanwhile the populace of Alexandria ran to the rescue of the governor, and put the rest of the monks to flight; but having secured Ammonius they delivered him up to the prefect. He immediately put him publicly to the torture, which was inflicted with such severity that he died under the effects of it: and not long after he [Orestes] gave an account to the emperors of what had taken place. Cyril on the other hand forwarded his statement of the matter to the emperor: and causing the body of Ammonius to be deposited in a certain church, he gave him the new appelation of Thaumasius [the admirable], ordering him to be enrolled among the martyrs, and eulogizing his magnanimity in church as that of one who had fallen in a conflict in defence of piety. But the more sober-minded, although Christians, did not accept Cyril's prejudiced estimation of him; for they well knew that he had suffered the punishment due to his rashness, and that he had not lost his life under the torture because he would not deny Christ. And Cyril himself being conscious of this, suffered the recollection of the circumstance to be gradually obliterated by silence. But the animosity between Cyril and Orestes did not by any means subside at this point, but was [kindled] afresh by an occurrence similar to the preceding.

## 3. Ibid., Chapter XV

*Of Hypatia the Female Philosopher.*

There was a woman at Alexandria named Hypatia, daughter of the philosopher Theon, who made such attainments in literature and science as to far surpass all the philosophers of her own time. Having succeeded to the school of Plato and Plotinus, she explained the principles of philosophy to her auditors, many of whom came from a distance to receive her instructions. On account of her self-possession and ease of manner, which she had acquired in consequence of the cultivation of her mind, she not infrequently appeared in public in the presence of the magistrates. Neither did she feel abashed in coming to an assembly of men. For all men on account of her extraordinary dignity and virtue admired her the more. Yet even she fell a victim to the political jealousy which at that time prevailed. For as she had frequent interviews with Orestes, it was calumniously reported among the Christian populace, that it was she who prevented Orestes from being reconciled to the bishop. Some of them therefore, hurried away by a fierce and bigoted zeal, whose ringleader was a reader named Peter, waylaid her returning home, and dragging her from her carriage, they took her to the church named *Caesareum*, where they completely stripped her, and then murdered her with [roofing] tiles [or oystershells]. After tearing her body in pieces, they took her mangled limbs to a place called Cinaron, and there burnt them. The affair brought not the least [i.e., considerable] opprobrium, not only on Cyril, but also on the whole Alexandrian church. And surely nothing can be further from the spirit of Christianity than the allowance of massacres, fights, and transactions of that sort. This happened in the month of March during

Lent, in the fourth year of Cyril's episcopate, under the tenth consulate of Honorius, and the sixth of Theodosius.

# C. JOHN OF NIKIU

## The Chronicle of John of Nikiu, *Chapter LXXXIV, §§ 87-103*

And in those days there appeared in Alexandria a female philosopher, a pagan named Hypatia, and she was devoted at all times to magic, astrolabes and instruments of music, and she beguiled many people through [her] satanic wiles. And the governor of the city honored her exceedingly; for she had beguiled him through her magic. And he ceased attending church as had been his custom. [But he went once under circumstances of danger.] And he not only did this, but he drew many believers to her, and he himself received the unbelievers at his house. And on a certain day when they were making merry over a theatrical exhibition connected with [dancers], the governor of the city [and he] published [an edict] [regarding] the public exhibitions in the city of Alexandria: and all the inhabitants of the city had assembled there [in the theatre]. Now Cyril, who had been appointed patriarch after Theophilus, was eager to gain exact intelligence regarding this edict. And there was a man named Hierax, a Christian possessing understanding and intelligence, who used to mock the pagans but was a devoted adherent of the illustrious Father the patriarch and was obedient to his monitions. He was also well versed in the Christian faith. [Now this man attended the theatre to learn the nature of this edict.] But when the Jews saw him in the theatre they cried out and said: 'This man has not come with any good purpose, but only to provoke an uproar.' And Orestes the prefect was displeased with the children of the holy church, and had Hierax seized and subjected to punishment publicly in the theatre, although he was wholly guiltless. And Cyril was wroth with the governor of the city for so doing, and likewise for his putting to death an illustrious monk of the convent of Pernôdj [Nitria]

named Ammonius, and other monks [also]. And when the [patriarch]
of the city heard this, he sent word to the Jews as follows: 'Cease your
hostilities against the Christians.' But they refused to hearken to what
they heard; for they gloried in the support of the prefect who was with
them, and so they added outrage to outrage and plotted a massacre
through a treacherous device. And they posted beside them at night in
all the streets of the city certain men, while others cried out and said:
'The church of the apostolic Athanasius is on fire: come to its succor,
all ye Christians.' And the Christians on hearing their cry came forth
quite ignorant of the treachery of the Jews. And when the Christians
came forth, the Jews arose and wickedly massacred the Christians and
shed the blood of many, guiltless though they were. And in the
morning, when the surviving Christians heard of the wicked deed
which the Jews had wrought, they betook themselves to the patriarch.
And the Christians mustered all together and went and marched in
wrath to the synagogues of the Jews and took possession of them, and
purified them and converted them into churches. [And one of them
they named after the name of S. George.] And as for the Jewish assas-
sins they expelled them from the city, and pillaged all their possessions
and drove them forth wholly despoiled, and Orestes the prefect was
unable to render them any help. And thereafter a multitude of believers
in God arose under the guidance of Peter the magistrate—now this
Peter was a perfect believer in all respects in Jesus Christ—and they
proceeded to seek for the pagan woman who had beguiled the people
of the city and the prefect through her enchantments. And when they
learned the place where she was they proceeded to her and found her
seated on a [lofty] chair; and having made her descend they dragged
her along till they brought her to the great church, named Caesarion.
Now this was in the days of the fast. And they tare off her clothing and
dragged her [till they brought her] through the streets of the city till she
died. And they carried her to a place named Cinaron, and they burned
her body with fire. And all the people surrounded the patriarch Cyril
and named him 'the new Theophilus'; for he had destroyed the last
remains of idolatry in the city.

# D. SYNESIUS OF CYRENE

## 1. To the Philosopher (Hypatia)

I salute you, and I beg of you to salute your most happy comrades for me, august Mistress. I have long been reproaching you that I am not deemed worthy of a letter, but now I know that I am despised by you all for no wrongdoing on my part, but because I am unfortunate in many things, in as many as a man can be. If I could only have had letters from you and learnt how you were all faring—I am sure you are happy and enjoying good fortune—I should have been relieved, in that case, of half my own trouble, in rejoicing at your happiness. But now your silence has been added to the sum of my sorrows. I have lost my children, my friends, and the goodwill of everyone. The greatest loss of all, however, is the absence of your divine spirit. I had hoped that this would always remain to me, to conquer both the caprices of fortune and the evil turns of fate.

## 2. To the Philosopher (Hypatia)

I am in such evil fortune that I need a hydroscope. See that one is cast in brass for me and put together. The instrument in question is a cylindrical tube, which has the shape of a flute and is about the same size. It has notches in a perpendicular line, by means of which we are able to test the weight of the waters. A cone forms a lid at one of the extremities, closely fitted to the tube. The cone and the tube have one base only. This is called the baryllium. Whenever you place the tube in water, it remains erect. You can then count the notches at your ease, and in this way ascertain the weight of the water.

## 3. To the Philosopher (Hypatia)

I am dictating this letter to you from my bed, but may you receive it in good health, mother, sister, teacher, and withal benefactress, and whatsoever is honored in name and deed. For me bodily weakness has followed in the wake of mental suffering. The remembrance of my departed children is consuming my forces, little by little. Only so long should Synesius have lived as he was still without experience of the evils of life. It is as if a torrent long pent up had burst upon me in full volume, and as if the sweetness of life had vanished. May I either cease to live, or cease to think of the tomb of my sons! But may you preserve your health and give my salutations to your happy comrades in turn, beginning with father Theotecnus and brother Athanasius, and so to all! And if anyone has been added to these, so long as he is dear to you, I must owe him gratitude because he is dear to you, and to that man give my greetings as to my own dearest friend. If any of my affairs interests you, you do well, and if any of them does not so interest you, neither does it me.

## 4. To the Philosopher (Hypatia)

I seemed destined to play the part of an echo. Whatever sounds I catch, these I repeat. I now pass on to you the praises of the marvellous Alexander. . . .

## 5. To the Philosopher (Hypatia)

Even if Fortune is unable to take everything away from me, at least she wants to take away everything that she can, she who has 'bereft me of my excellent sons'. But she can never take away from me the choice of the best, and the power to come to the help of the oppressed, for never may she prevail to change my heart! I abhor iniquity: for one may, and I would fain prevent it, but this also is one of those things which were taken from me; this went even before my children.

'Aforetime the Milesians were men of might.' There was a time when I, too, was of some use to my friends. You yourself called me the providence of others. All respect which was accorded to me by the mighty of this earth I employed solely to help others. The great were merely my instruments. But now, alas, I am deserted and abandoned by all, unless *you* have some power to help. I account you as the only good thing that remains inviolate, along with virtue. You always have power, and long may you have it and make good use of that power. I recommend to your care Nicaeus and Philolaus, two excellent young men united by the bond of relationship. In order that they may come again into possession of their own property, try to get support for them from all your friends, whether private individuals or magistrates.

## 6. To the Philosopher (Hypatia)

Even though there shall be utter forgetfulness of the dead in Hades 'even there shall I remember thee,' my dear Hypatia. I am encompassed by the sufferings of my city, and disgusted with her, for I daily see the enemy forces, and men slaughtered like victims on an altar. I am breathing an air tainted by the decay of dead bodies. I am waiting to undergo myself the same lot that has befallen so many others, for how can one keep any hope, when the sky is obscured by the shadow of birds of prey? Yet even under these conditions I love the country. Why then do I suffer? Because I am a Libyan, because I was born here, and it is here that I see the honoured tombs of my ancestors. On your account alone I think I should be capable of overlooking my city, and changing my abode, if ever I had the chance of doing so.

## 7. To the Philosopher (Hypatia)

I have brought out two books this year. One of them as I was moved thereto by God Himself, the other because of the slander of men. Some of those who wear the white or dark mantle have maintained that I am faithless to philosophy, apparently because I profess grace and harmony of style, and because I venture to say something concerning Homer and concerning the figures of the rhetoricians. In the eyes of such persons one must hate literature in order to be a philosopher, and must occupy himself with divine matters only. No doubt these men alone have become spectators of the knowable. This privilege is unlawful for me, for I spend some of my leisure in purifying my tongue and sweetening my wit. The thing which urged them to condemn me, on the charge that I am fit only for trifling, is the fact that my *Cynegetics* disappeared from my house, how I know not, and that they have been received with great enthusiasm by certain young men who make a cult of Atticisms and graceful periods. Moreover, some poetical attempts of mine have seemed to them to be the work of an artist who reproduces the antique, as we are wont to say in speaking of statues. There are certain men among my critics whose effrontery is only surpassed by their ignorance, and these are the readiest of all to spin out discussions concerning God. Whenever you meet them, you have to listen to their babble about inconclusive syllogisms. They pour a torrent of phrases over those who stand in no need of them, in which I suppose they find their own profit. The public teachers that one sees in our cities, come from this class. It is the very Horn of Amalthea which they think themselves entitled to use. You will, I think, recognize this easy-going tribe, which miscalls nobility of purpose. They wish me to become their pupil; they say that in a short time they will make me all-daring in questions of divinity, and that I shall be able to declaim day and night without stopping. The rest, who have more taste, are, as sophists, much more unfortunate than these. They would like to be famous in the same way, but fortunately for them they are incapable even of this. You know some who, despoiled at the office of the tax collector, or urged thereto by some one calamity, have become philosophers in the middle of their lives. Their philosophy consists in a very simple formula, that of calling God to witness, as Plato did, whenever they deny anything or whenever they assert anything. A shadow would surpass these men in uttering anything to the point; but their pretensions are extraordinary. Oh, what proudly arched brows! They support the heads with the hand. They assume a more solemn countenance than the statues of Xenocrates. They are even resolved to shackle us with a law that is altogether to their advantage; to wit, that no one shall be in open possession of any knowledge of the good.

They esteem it an exposure of themselves if any one, deemed a philosopher, knows how to speak, for they think to hide behind a veil of simulation and to appear to be quite full of wisdom within. These are the two types of men who have falsely charged me with occupying myself in trivial pursuits, one of them because I do not talk the same sort of nonsense as they do, the other because I do not keep my mouth shut, and do not keep the 'bull on my tongue' as they do. Against these was my treatise composed, and it deals with the loquacity of one school and the silence of the other. Although it is to the latter in particular that it is addressed, namely to the speechless and envious men in question (do you not think with some comeliness of form?), none the less it has found means of dragging in those other men also, and it aims at being not less an exhibition than an encomium of great learning. Nor did I abjure their charges, but for their still greater discomfiture I have even courted them.

Next, passing to the choice of a life, the work praises that of philosophy as being the most philosophic of choices; and what sort of choice it must be regarded, learn from the book itself. Finally, it defends my library also, which some men have accused, on the ground that it conceals unrevised copies. The spiteful fellows have not kept their hands even off things like these. If each thing is in its proper place; and all things have been handled in season; if the motives behind each part of the undertaking are just; if it has been divided into a number of chapters in the manner of that divine work *The Phaedrus*, in which Plato discusses the various types of the beautiful; if all the arguments have been devised to converge on the one end proposed; if, moreover, conviction has anywhere quietly come to the support of the flatness of the narrative, and if out of conviction demonstration has resulted, as happens in such cases, and if one thing follows from another logically, these results must be gifts of nature and art.

He who is not undisciplined to discover even a certain divine countenance hidden under a coarser model, like that of Aphrodite, those Graces, and such charming divinities as the Athenian artists concealed within sculptured figures of a Silenus or a Satyr, that man, at all events, will apprehend all that my book has unveiled of the mystic dogmas. But the meanings of these will easily escape others because of their semblance of redundancy, and their appearance of being thrown into the narrative too much by chance, and as it might seem roughly. Epileptics are the only people who feel the cold influences of the moon. On the other hand only those receive the flashes of the emanations of the intellect, for whom in the full health of the mind's eye God kindles a light akin to his own, that light which is the cause of knowledge to the intellectual, and to knowable things the cause of their being known. In the same way, ordinary light connects sight with color. But remove this light, and its power to discern is ineffective.

Concerning all this I shall await your decision. If you decree that I ought to publish my book, I will dedicate it to orators and philosophers together. The first it will please, and to the others it will be useful, provided of course that it is not rejected by you, who are really able to pass judgment. If it does not seem to you worthy of Greek ears, if, like Aristotle, you prize truth more than friendship, a close and profound darkness will overshadow it, and mankind will never hear it mentioned.

So much for this matter. The other work God ordained and He gave His sanction to it, and it has been set up as a thank-offering to the imaginative faculties. It contains an inquiry into the whole imaginative soul, and into some other points which have not yet been handled by any Greek philosopher. But why should one dilate on this? This work was completed, the whole of it, in a single night, or rather, at the end of a night, one which also brought the vision enjoining me to write it. There are two or three passages in the book in which it seemed to me that I was some other person, and that I was one listening to myself amongst others who were present. Even now this work, as often as I go over it, produces a marvellous effect upon me, and a certain divine voice envelops me as in poetry. Whether this my experience is not unique, or may happen to another, on all this you will enlighten me, for after myself you will be the first of the Greeks to have access to the work. The books that I am sending you have not yet been published, and in order that the number may be complete, I am sending you also my essay concerning the Gift. This was produced long ago in my ambassadorial period. It was addressed to a man who had great influence with the emperor, and Pentapolis profited somewhat from the essay, and also from the gift.

### 8. To His Brother (an excerpt)

[The letter, a long one, describes a voyage beset by storm and resulting in shipwreck. Only its conclusion is here relevant.]

. . . Farewell; give my kindest messages to your son Dioscorus and to his mother and grandmother, both of whom I love and look upon as though they were my own sisters. Salute for me the most holy and revered philosopher [Hypatia], and give my homage also to the company of the blessed who delight in her oracular utterance. Above all to the worthy and holy Theotecnus, and my friend, Athanasius. As to our most sympathetic Gaius, I well know that you, like myself, regard him as a member of our family. Do not forget to remember me to them, as also to Theodosius, who is not merely a grammarian of the first order, but one who, if he really be a diviner, has certainly succeeded in deceiving us. He surely must have foreseen the incidents of this voyage, for he finally gave up his desire to come with me. However, that is a matter that does not signify. I love and embrace him. As for you, may you never trust yourself at sea, or at least, if you really must do so, let it not be at the end of a month.

### 9. To Olympius (an excerpt)

[This is a reply which begins by acknowledging receipt of a long-delayed letter. It suggests new arrangements for delivery and goes on to describe the difficult situation in which he is placed, fearing the hostility of a besieging army. Only a short passage is relevant here.]

... I shall ... arrange things differently in future, and entrust [my letters] to Peter alone. I think Peter will bring on this letter through the agency of the sacred hand, for I am sending it from Pentapolis to our common teacher [Hypatia]. She will choose the man by whom she wishes it to be conveyed, and her choice, I am sure, will fall upon the most trusted messenger. ...

## 10. To His Brother (an excerpt)

[The burden of this letter is his disappointment with Athens. He ends
by comparing it unfavorably with Alexandria.]

... To-day Egypt has received and cherishes the fruitful wisdom of Hypatia. Athens was aforetime the dwelling-place of the wise: to-day the bee-keepers alone bring it honor. Such is the case of that pair of sophists in Plutarch who draw the young people to the lecture room—not by fame of their eloquence, but by pots of honey from Hymettus.

## 11. To Herculian (an excerpt)

[Herculian was a close friend and fellow student of Synesius. This
letter is a lengthy protestation of friendship and of mutual dedication
to philosophy. It contains the following passage.]

... We have seen with our eyes, we have heard with our ears the lady [Hypatia] who legitimately presides over the mysteries of philosophy. And if human interests join those who share them in a bond of union, so a divine law demands of us who are united in mind, which is the best part of us, to honor each other's qualities. ...

## 12. An excerpt from De Dono Astrolabii (addressed to Paeonius)

[The bulk of this long letter flatters Paeonius. It accompanied the gift
of an astrolabe to that official, "a military man who was fond of phi-

losophy, science, and literature." It gives considerable detail on the history of the instrument and also provides some details of its theory, construction, and use. Immediately after the passage quoted in chapter 6, we find the following words.]

. . . I am therefore offering you a gift most befitting for me to give, and for you to receive. It is a work of my own devising, including all that she, my most revered teacher [Hypatia], helped to contribute, and it was executed by the best hand to be found in our country in the art of the silversmiths. . . .

# E. MISCELLANEOUS

## 1. Theon's Inscription, Book III of his Commentary on Ptolemy's Almagest

Theon of Alexandria's commentary on the third [book] of the Mathematical Syntaxis of Ptolemy, the edition having been prepared by the philosopher, my daughter Hypatia.

## 2. From Philostorgius's Ecclesiasticae Historiae, Liber VIII, § B θ ′

Well does he [Philostorgius] say that Hypatia the daughter of Theon was taught mathematics by her father, but reached an excellence far above her teacher, especially in astronomy, and that she instructed many [pupils] in mathematical studies. However, the ungodly man states that she was torn to pieces by the homöousians [orthodox Christians] during the reign of Theodosius the Younger.

## 3. From The Chronicle of John Malalas, Book 14, § 12

At that time, the Alexandrians, given free rein by their bishop, seized and burnt on a pyre of brushwood Hypatia the famous philosopher, who had a great reputation and who was an old woman.

## 4. Excerpt from Theophanes' Chronographia § 71

In this year [406 CE], some people brought about the death, the violent death, of Hypatia, the daughter of Theon the philosopher, and herself given to philosophical endeavors.

# NOTES

References not given in full are listed in the Annotated Bibliography.

## INTRODUCTION

I have not deemed it necessary to detail every single reference to Hypatia that may be discovered by a sufficiently diligent reader, nor to criticize in their minutiae the faults of the many bad ones. However, it does need to be said, because of the work's overall authority, that the relevant entry in the *Dictionary of Scientific Biography* is below the general standard of its articles. And it also needs to be said, because in this case of the work's wide distribution and misleadingly reassuring imprint, that L. Osen's *Women in Mathematics* (Cambridge, MA: MIT Press, 1974) is a dreadful book and the chapter on Hypatia perhaps its worst. I refrain from discussion of its (many) specific flaws. They should be obvious to any careful reader.

At any given time various biographies circulate on the Internet. Their quality varies, but is generally poor. Two of the worst, both versions of an attempt to plagiarize Deakin (1994), have now mercifully been removed. Of the others, one of the better ones http://www-groups.dcs.st-and.ac.uk/~history /Mathematicians/Hypatia.html is nonetheless rather unsatisfactory, being very scrappy as well as inaccurate in places, though it does have the virtue of stressing Hypatia's status as a *mathematician*. The best of the material on the Internet was to be found via Landman's site, http://www.polyamory.org /~howard/Hypatia/ and the links given there, many of which are now inactive. Far too much of what is brought up with a Google search derives directly from Osen, and thus has no credence. However, such material changes almost daily. These comments applied in March 2007.

There are, on the other hand, four short works I would explicitly exempt from my general condemnation of readily available material. These are Duckett (1972), Mueller (1987), Waithe (1987), and chapter 11 of Knorr (1989). Mueller (1987) is a short but excellent article with a first-rate annotated bibliography. Duckett (1972) and Waithe (1987) are more extended pieces, and they can both be recommended (but modulo quite a few quibbles), although only Waithe (1987) attempts to deal in any detail with Hypatia's mathematics. Knorr (1989) is a very detailed, if speculative, study that is considered more fully in chapter 9 of this book. It is perhaps appropriate also to mention the short article by McCabe (1903), which, although not easy to come by and written explicitly to counter Kingsley, is quite sensible.

In a separate category is a recent book-length biography by Dzielska (1995). This devotes much of its space to the legends but also gives scholarly attention to aspects of Hypatia's life. There is a brave, but quite unsatisfactory, attempt to discuss the mathematics; however, other aspects of this work are very good. By and large the conclusions reached are consonant with those favored here.

Dora Russell's book *Hypatia, or Women and Knowledge* (London: Kegan Paul, 1925) is not concerned with the life or thought of Hypatia.

The relevant passage in Gibbon's *Decline and Fall* is to be found in its chapter 47.

Kingsley's novel is still widely available and has gone through many editions from its first publication in 1851. I doubt that today it is much read. (Kingsley seems to be in eclipse, although *The Water-Babies* and possibly *Westward Ho!* still retain some vogue.) The artistic merits of the novel have been variously assessed and the reader may care to see how critical opinion has regarded it by comparing different editions of *The Oxford Companion to English Literature*.

The novel is avowedly that—though Kingsley was a not inconsiderable historian, and his preface does claim to be a work of scholarship. Regrettably, even that contains a number of arbitrary and unexplained judgments that should have no place in such a work. For more detail, see, for example, Rhys's introduction to the Everyman edition. The novel was a source of great controversy when it first appeared and so there are many discussions of its historical accuracy, but as it makes no claim to be anything other than fiction and is now hardly ever read, we can safely ignore all of this.

Asmus (1907) lists several other such literary uses of the Hypatia story—they will be even less familiar to most readers and I similarly overlook them, as also those further works of the same ilk that have appeared in the years since Asmus's article. Readers interested in this aspect of the matter will also find much material in Dzielska's (1995) book.

The most usually reproduced "portrait" of Hypatia is Gasparo's, whose modern currency dates from its use in the *Little Journeys* series (vol. 23, pt. 4). (The cover portrait is Gasparo's.) These volumes were put out by the American eccentric Elbert Hubbard around the end of the nineteenth century. This particular one dealt with Hypatia, appeared in 1908, and was (until its recent appearance on the Internet, via Landman's site, given above) very rare outside the United States; its general tenor and its overall ahistoricity may also be gauged from the extensive quotes in Osen's book, *Women in Mathematics*. It is essentially a work of fiction. Hubbard is in fact Osen's main source.

Other "portraits" to have some currency are those in Halma (1822) and Toland ([1720] 1753). Neither can claim the artistic merit of Gasparo's, nor the care in attempting to re-create, in facial features and in clothing, some semblance of verisimilitude. The medallion on the first of the two title pages of Halma's book is not explicitly identified at all, but it is reasonable to assume it represents Hypatia. A reproduction is given by Richeson (1940) along with a good-quality reproduction of the Gasparo portrait. Richeson's article is probably the source for most subsequent reproductions of this latter. These three portraits are all reproduced in Deakin's (1994) paper. A fourth, by A. Seifert, is reproduced by Donald Viney, the editor of *Questions of Value: Readings for Basic Philosophy* (Needham Heights, MA: Ginn, 1989). Dzielska (1995) also notes a sculpture by the contemporary feminist artist Judy Chicago.

Other representations also exist. One, by Charles William Mitchell, has recently appeared on the Internet at http://en.wikipedia.org/wiki/Hypatia. It depicts a naked Hypatia cowering against an altar, presumably forced into this position by her (unseen) murderers. It is an English Victorian painting in an erotic style in vogue at the time; in fact, it has clear sado-erotic overtones. These derive directly from what Marrou (1964) calls a "purple passage" in Kingsley's novel. Marrou also mentions another illustration of this same passage, one by Lee Woodward Ziegler, and the charge of sado-eroticism applies here also. With the appearance of Mitchell's work on the Internet, readers may form their own opinions. Certainly one might say that the perpetrators of Hypatia's murder were sado-erotic in their intentions; however, this stricture need not apply to those who describe their despicable actions, unless they needlessly dwell upon prurient detail, as perhaps is the case here.

Another "portrait" derives from the imaginative suggestion that the so-called Fayum portraits depict the way Hypatia may have appeared. These are contemporary portraits of real-life Egyptian Hellenes from the right period. Of course, none of these are claimed to depict Hypatia herself, but they probably provide us with a guide as to how, in a general way, she may have looked. One is available at http://penelope.uchicago.edu/~grout/encyclopaedia_romana /greece/paganism/hypatia.html and a Google search under "Fayum portraits" will yield more.

A note on pronunciation may also be in order. Hypatia herself and her contemporaries probably pronounced her name something like *heew-pah-TEE-ah*, where my spelling of the first syllable is meant to approximate the German sound *hü*. English speakers often and unashamedly anglicize the sound to *high-PAY-shuh*, and I see nothing wrong with this. After all, we pronounce "Paris" as *PARR-us* or as *PAIR-us* and do not feel constrained to attempt the French pronunciation, which is closer to *par-HEE*. Other similar examples could be given.

# CHAPTER 1

The matters summarized here are drawn from a select group of widely available sources. There are useful articles on Alexandria in the *Britannica* and in the *New Catholic Encyclopedia* and I have also made extensive use of the former's article on ancient Rome. In addition, I have referred to Bury ([1893] 1958) but have not accepted his dates. Table 1 is a simplified version of part of the table in the *Britannica*.

The earlier history derives from the relevant articles in the *Britannica*, Eliade (1987), the *New Catholic Encyclopedia*, and the *Dictionary of Scientific Biography*. The basis of Plato's Academy is described in his *Republic*. Alexander's edict on the equality of Jews and Greeks is given in *The Cambridge History of Judaism*, vol. 2, ed. W. D. Davies and L. Finkelstein (Cambridge University Press, 1989), p. 120. For the antiquity of Jewish settlement in Alexandria, see also the extract from Socrates Scholasticus in appendix D, section B.

The early spread of Christianity in Egypt is documented by P. D. Scott-Moncrieff—in his *Paganism and Christianity in Egypt* (Cambridge University Press, 1913)—who casts doubt on the "Mark tradition." He also has some interesting background on the cult of Serapis.

That Greek remained the language of Alexandria after it became part of the Roman Empire is attested by the fact that the works from this period were all written in Greek. In fact, Hypatia's pupil Synesius knew no Latin. See Crawford (1901).

The two halves of the Roman Empire were briefly reunited under Theodosius I, but separated again on his death in 395. Thus, this latter date is sometimes given as the year of the split between the East and the West; in fact, I followed this convention myself in my earlier paper (Deakin 1994).

The destruction of the temple of Serapis is reported by both Socrates Scholasticus and Sozomen (see Zenos 1891). The date (or dates) of the destruction of the Museum and its libraries is more controversial. There is a brief discussion by Dzielska (1995). I here follow the account given in the *Britannica*.

For Cyril's character, see Thurstone and Attwater (1956) and Holweck (1924).

The expulsion of the Jews from Alexandria in 414 CE was actually temporary. See the *Encyclopedia Judaica*, vol. 4, p. 1550.

Theodosius's edict of 423 CE is given by H. H. Ben-Sasson: *A History of the Jewish People* (London: Weidenfeld and Nicholson, 1976).

For Anthemius and related matters, see Tannery (1880).

For a useful map of Alexandria at the relevant period, see the *New Catholic Encyclopedia* under "Alexandria."

# CHAPTER 2

The early part of the chapter I have based on the article "Alexandrian Schools" in the eleventh edition of the *Britannica*. I have corrected it in one respect by removing the name of Hipparchus (a pre-Ptolemaic astronomer) from its list of Alexandrian mathematicians. The *Dictionary of Scientific Biography*, under "Hipparchus," makes it clear that Hipparchus did not in fact go there.

The brief descriptions of the various mathematicians are all drawn from the *Dictionary of Scientific Biography*. For obvious reasons I have added the name of Theon of Alexandria to the list in the *Britannica* article.

*On the Measurement of the Circle* is the book that contains Archimedes' famous estimate of the value of the mathematical constant $\pi$.

Euclid, in fact, produced a work, now lost, the *Conics*. There has been much conjecture about what Euclid and other pre-Apollonian mathematicians knew on the subject. However, it is agreed that Apollonius's work was an outstanding advance on anything that went before.

For an account of the excellences of the Ptolemaic system of astronomy, Fred Hoyle's popular work *Nicolaus Copernicus: An Essay on His Life and Work* (London: Heinemann, 1973) will fill the bill nicely. It was devoted to showing the achievements of the Ptolemaic system and thus by implication those of the even better Copernican alternative. Following Copernicus, Kepler gave a more accurate description of the orbits of the planets about the sun, and it was this that led Newton to the discovery of the law of gravity.

The rise of the commentary as a genre was accompanied by a rapid decline in the production of independent research works. The last known such from the Greek tradition are two books by Serenus, which were produced in Egypt (but not in Alexandria) in possibly the fourth century CE. They are of poor quality. See Heath (1921).

The suggestion that Hypatia taught from her home is based on the account in the *Suda Lexicon* (see appendix D, section A, and Adler ([1935] 1971) and this is so interpreted by Asmus (1911) and Dzielska (1995).

The remainder of the chapter is based on the current edition of the *Britannica*, as well as on volume 1 of F. Coppleston's *A History of Philosophy* (London: Search, 1946), pp. 482–83; the *Dictionary of Scientific Biography*, the *New Catholic Encyclopedia*, Eliade (1987), and Crawford (1901).

It should not need to be said that Ptolemy the astronomer (and geographer) is a different man from Ptolemy I Soter. They are quite distinct, although they share a family name. Similarly Ammonius Saccas is not the Ammonius who turns up in chapter 7. Both are different again from the later philosopher Ammonius, who also taught in Alexandria, but long after Hypatia's death. However, the Proclus mentioned toward the end of the chapter is one man who appears first as a mathematician and later as a philosopher.

The destruction of the Museum around 390 is attested by a contemporary description by Epiphanius (not the Epiphanius of Theon's dedications discussed in chapter 5). For details, see Mueller (1987).

# CHAPTER 3

## Section A

The principal sources for this section are the relevant articles in the *New Catholic Encyclopedia* and Eliade (1987). The descriptions of the various heretical groups also rely on Blunt (1874). For material on Cyril, see Thurstone and Attwater (1956), Farmer (1978), and Holweck (1924). Cyril's extant works are reprinted in ten volumes of the *Patrologiae Graecae* (Migne 1857–1866).

## Section B

The sources are the *New Catholic Encyclopedia*, Eliade (1987), and the *Dictionary of Scientific Biography*. That mathematicians tend, as a working philosophy, to adopt a naive Platonism is deplored by contemporary mathematician Philip J. Davis (see, for example, *American Mathematical Monthly* 79 [1972]: 252–63), who, however, succeeds in documenting very well that this is the case.

Iamblichus's generation of numbers from the One strikes a chord with modern mathematicians familiar with the Peano axioms and other such derivations of the number system. However, it would be quite anachronistic to attribute any such technical advance to Iamblichus. A somewhat similar point could be made in respect of his use of points to generate lines, curves, surfaces, and other geometric objects.

## Section C

This section relies almost entirely on the *New Catholic Encyclopedia*, especially its article on Porphyry. However, for a much fuller account, giving much more detail than is relevant here, see Bregman (1982). There is also valuable material in Duckett (1972).

The Platonist thought of Philo Judaeus has already been noted in chapter 1. This is sometimes seen as giving a Trinitarian structure to the Hebrew God, but (necessarily) without invoking an incarnation as in section A above.

The account of the doctrine of the Trinity presented in section A is one centered on humankind and its routes to God; that presented in this section makes the triune nature of God an intrinsic property of the deity, independent of any human knowledge. Trinitarian *formulae* (as distinct from developed theology) are found very early in Christian writing (e.g., Logion 44 of the extracanonical Gospel of Thomas, which some have dated as early as 60 CE).

# CHAPTER 4

A useful, accessible, and modern summary of source material and its relevance is given by Mueller (1987). However, other less easily available sources, especially Wernsdorf (1747/8), Wolf (1879), Bigoni (1886/7), and Asmus (1907), often provide more detail. Primary source material is reprinted, translated, and paraphrased by Asmus (1911), Fabricius (1718), Schmidt (1691), Sextus ([n.d.] 1843), Seeck (1966), Wolfius (1739), and in the *Patrologiae Graecae* (Migne 1857–1866). Extensive quotations from primary sources occur throughout Dzielska's (1995) work.

The question as to what extent Hypatia "revised" Theon's work in Book III of the Commentary on the *Almagest* is by no means settled. Knorr (1989) and others ascribe the present version to Hypatia herself. Cameron (1990) assigns her a much lesser role. It is also in dispute whether her influence is to be found in the subsequent books of this work. The translation in appendix D, section E, is that of Knorr (1989); the one quoted in the text is a slight variant of that given by Heath (1938). For more detail, see chapter 9.

For information on the *Suda Lexicon*, see *The Oxford Companion to Classical Literature*, 2nd ed. (Oxford University Press, 1985), 54. The sources of its entry on Hypatia are variously discussed. In the main, I have followed Tannery (1880), but Praechter's article on Hypatia in *Paulys Realencyclopädie* has a careful discussion of the matter, which is also considered in depth by Flach (1882) and by Asmus (1911). The edition of the *Suda* used in my work is Adler's ([1935] 1971), but most of the relevant passages are also given by Zintzen (1967), who, however, regards the attribution of much of it to Damascius as doubtful.

For information on Hesychius and the *Onomatologus*, see again Flach (1882) or, more accessibly, the *Tusculum Lexicon,* 3rd ed. (Munich: Artemis, 1982), 336–37, and the entry Hesychios 10 in *Paulys Realencyclopädie.*

A sentence believed to be by Damascius, casting some aspersion on Hypatia and not included in the *Suda,* is to be found in the *Patrologiae Graecae,* vol. 103, cols. 1285–86 (Migne 1857–1866). It will be discussed in detail in later chapters. See also appendix D, section A.4.

The relevant passages from Socrates Scholasticus are also to be found in Migne (1857–1866, vol. 67). Hypatia is referred to directly in columns 767–70, and earlier material—also included here in appendix D, section B— is usually held to be highly germane. See also Migne (1857–1866, vol. 66, cols. 1047–48).

The passage from Philostorgius is to be found in Migne (1857–1866, vol. 65, cols. 563–64). The English translation in appendix D, section E, is my own from the Latin version given there, but correcting it in one minor respect. Mueller (1987) mentions a previously published English translation, but it has not been available to me.

The sentence from Malalas is in Migne's compendium (1857–1866, vol. 97, cols. 535–36). Those from Nicephoras Gregoras are to be found there also (Migne 1857–1866, vol. 148, cols. 469–70 and vol. 149, cols. 529–30). The brief notice in Theophanes' *Chronographia* is likewise there (Migne 1857–1866, vol. 108, cols. 225–26). The translation from Malalas given in appendix D, section E, is that of E. Jeffreys et al. from *The Chronicle of John Malalas* (Melbourne: Australian Association for Byzantine Studies, 1986). That of Theophanes is my own from the Latin version in Migne (1857–1866). Halma (1822) gives a French, and Wolf (1879) a German, rendering.

Mueller (1987) and Dzielska (1995) were the first and for some time almost the only authors to point to the passage in John of Nikiu's *Chronicle* (Charles [1916] 1981?). However, it is now available on several Web sites, so that it is today much better known than before. (I learned of it first from Mueller [1987]. This is but one of the many debts I owe to his excellent article.) That Nikiu's account derives in the main from Socrates' is most clearly demonstrated by the fact that both authors, having discussed Hypatia's death, then move on to the same unrelated tale of Jewish "atrocities"—in faraway Syria. It should however be pointed out, see appendix D, sections B and C, that in the retelling Socrates' account has become garbled, and that some other source must also be involved—instance the reference to the astrolabe.

Synesius's letters are to be found in Migne (1857–1866, vol. 66, cols. 1321–1560). The vexed question of their numbering is now one that requires careful attention. Table 2 on page 172 summarizes the eleven letters involving Hypatia and lists the numbers given to them by various authors. Its sources are Roques (1989) and FitzGerald (1926). Because Migne's (1857–1866) numbering contains several errors due to some earlier miscounting, other writers, even those who have wished to use it as standard, have felt constrained to modify it. It has nothing but custom to recommend it and it bears no relation to dates of composition. The best estimates of these dates are those of Roques (1989), also given in table 2. FitzGerald's translations have been criticized, although not in any respect that is relevant here—see, for instance, Neugebauer (1949)—but they are the standard English versions and for this reason are those given here in appendix D. Other passages of translation occur throughout Dzielska's (1995) book.

Cassiodorus's translation is given in *Patrologiae Graecae* (Migne 1857–1866) and is also to be found in the companion *Patrologiae Latinae*, vol. 69 (Paris: Migne, 1865), cols. 1193–95. For Callistus, see Migne (1857–1866, vol. 146, cols. 1105–1106). The alleged letter from Hypatia to Cyril is printed twice in Migne (1857–1866, vol. 77, cols. 389–90 and vol. 84, col. 848). It represents Hypatia as sympathetic to the Nestorian cause. Dzielska (1995) gives an English translation.

| GARYZA | PG | FITZGERALD | HERCHER | DRUON | DATE |
|---|---|---|---|---|---|
| 1 | 10 | 10 | 10 | 10 | 156 | EARLY 413 |
| 2 | 15 | 15 | 15 | 14bis | 52 | EARLY 413 |
| 3 | 16 | 16 | 16 | 16 | 157 | EARLY 413 |
| 4 | 46 | 33 | 33 | 33 | 2 | 405 OR 406 |
| 5 | 81 | 80 | 81 | 81 | 154 | EARLY 413 |
| 6 | 124 | 124 | 124 | 124 | 24 | MAY ? 405 |
| 7 | 154 | 153 | 154 | 154 | 63 | LATE 404 |
| 8 | 5 | 4 | 4 | 4 | 16 | 23 OCT 407 |
| 9 | 133 | 132 | 133 | 133 | 73 | MAY 405 |
| 10 | 136 | 135 | 136 | 136 | 13 | AUG. 399 |
| 11 | 137 | 136 | 137 | 137 | 4 | EARLY 398 |

**Table 2.** Synesius's letters as listed by various editors. The first column gives the letter as headed in appendix D of this book; the second as listed by A. Garyza, *Epistolae Synesii Cyrenensis* (Rome: Istituto Poligrafico, 1979); the third gives the numbering in Migne (1857–1866); the fourth as listed by FitzGerald (1926); the fifth the numbering assigned by R. Hercher, *Epistolographi Graeci* (Paris: Didot, 1873); the sixth the numbering of H. Druon's French edition *Œuvres de Synésios* (Paris: Durand, 1878). This last attempted to reflect the historical order of the letters, but it has been superseded in this regard by Roques (1989), given above in the final column. The numbering used by Roques (1989) is that of Garyza. This table is based on a similar one in Roques (1989). It should be noted that Dzielska (1995) does not always accept Roques's dates.

The epigram of which an English translation appears after my title page is usually although not conclusively attributed to Palladas. See, for example, Wolfius (1739), pp. 91–92. The Greek original and an English prose translation are to be found in *The Greek Anthology*, vol. 3, trans. W. R. Paton (Loeb Classical Library; London: Heinemann, 1917), 222–23. The English translation printed here is from Toland ([1720] 1753). The epigram is not, of course, strictly speaking a primary source, although it is sometimes listed, for example, by Wolfius (1739), as being one. It attests to the regard in which Hypatia was held, and that is all. Palladas was, however, an Alexandrine contemporary of Hypatia, and so, if he did write the epigram and if it did refer to her and not to some namesake, it was a contemporary tribute. But Palladas's authorship, it should be noted, is by no means assured or agreed; Wernsdorf (1747/8), for example, attributes the verse to Paulus Silentarius, who lived almost two hundred years later. For an extensive and accessible discussion, see Dzielska (1995). Toland's translation, while it works well as English verse, fails to preserve the form of the original. The best attempt to keep both form and sense in an English rendering is that of Duckett (1972).

# CHAPTER 5

The first modern attempt to date Hypatia's death accurately is that of Baronius (1601). Prior to this, the date 406 given by Theophanes (Migne 1857–1866, vol. 108, cols. 225–26) had been accepted. The first full and detailed discussion is that given by Wernsdorf (1747/8), but most readers will find the more concise accounts by Hoche (1860) and, even more so, Seeck (1966) the more readily accessible. There is still some disagreement as to whether Hypatia died in 415 or 416. Baronius (1601), after an unjustified alteration to the text of Socrates Scholasticus, and Hoche (1860) adopt the former date, but Wernsdorf (1747/8), in large part, Seeck (1966), and indeed Wolf (1879) opt for the second. In this they are today very much in a minority, although their accounts are the more elaborated. A simple formulaic approach to the correction of Theophanes' date yields 414, but this is not an accurate way to proceed. For more detail, see Wernsdorf (1747/8). Because there is such widespread *general* agreement, however, on the date of Hypatia's death, I have not felt it necessary to enter into a fuller discussion. I was, however, more than a little surprised to see that Dzielska (1995) accepts the 415 date without comment.

Modern consular lists (e.g., *Consuls of the Later Roman Empire* by R. S. Bagnall, A. Cameron, S. R. Schwartz, and K. A. Worp [Atlanta, GA: American Philological Association, 1987] and A. Capelli's *Cronologia, Cronografia e Calendario Perpetuo*, 5th ed. [Milan: Hoepli, 1978]) unambiguously give the calendric equivalent of the consular date as 415 and thus are at odds with Seeck's contention that there is source for error in the consular records on this point. Thus the discrepancy between secular and ecclesiastical records is explained by those espousing the 415 date as arising either from arithmetic error (as suggested in the text) or else by positing that Cyril counted the years of his see from the first of January (which in practice amounts to the same thing).

When we come to Hypatia's birth, because much less is known and agreed on the matter, I elaborate more. The question is discussed in many of the secondary sources. Mueller (1987) gives a brief summary, and I have tended to follow his line of thought. Hoche (1860) discusses the matter at length, as do Bigoni (1886/7), Crawford (1901), Wernsdorf (1747/8), and Wolf (1879); also relevant are the entries on Theon and on Pappus in the *Dictionary of Scientific Biography*. The earlier date for her birth is advanced by Wernsdorf (1747/8), whose account set a standard for scholarship that was not bettered for nearly 250 years.

Another item of evidence may perhaps be adduced in favor of the earlier date for Hypatia's birth. Philostorgius's account of Hypatia immediately precedes a narration of events under Valentinian and Valens. This (see chapter 1, table 1) would seem to make her active in the early 370s. Wolf (1879) and McCabe (1903) take this route, but it is not a very convincing argument given the poorly preserved state of Philostorgius's text.

For a further careful study of the date of Hypatia's birth, see Penella (1984), who discounts the later date, but himself offers no firm speculation. This is much the approach of the present study, except that I am perhaps a little more inclined than he to think that 370 is too late. Dzielska (1995) takes a similar view.

The texts giving Hypatia's parentage are to be found in appendix D. The translation of Theon's inscription given there is that of Knorr (1989). However, Cameron (1990) interprets matters differently. But although translations of this text indeed vary considerably, all recognize the father-daughter relationship. For further discussion, see chapter 9.

The dates of the eclipses observed by Theon have been calculated independently by many different investigators, beginning with Halma and ending with Tihon. We may take it that these results are set in concrete. I quote Tihon's (1978) version, which offers the most minuscule of addenda to the more accessible account given by Toomer in his article on Theon in the *Dictionary of Scientific Biography*. For the 320 eclipse, I have simply accepted Bulmer-Thomas's date from his article on Pappus in the same source. For an accessible account of the calculations involved in the prediction and dating of eclipses, see parts of Fred Hoyle's popular work *On Stonehenge* (San Francisco: Freeman, 1977).

The *Suda* entries on Theon and on Pappus are discussed by Toomer and by Bulmer-Thomas in their respective articles in the *Dictionary of Scientific Biography*, as is the general question of dating as precisely as possible the lives of these men. The "conjunction" of 377 is discussed by Tihon (1978). For an account of Theon's mathematical and astronomical works, see again Toomer's article in the *Dictionary of Scientific Biography*. I am here crediting him with three editions of Euclid and five commentaries on Ptolemy, including two works on the astrolabe. One of these commentaries, that on the *Almagest*, went to two editions.   See chapter 9, sections B and C, and appendix A, sections A and D.

For the impression given of Hypatia's age, see the extracts from the *Suda* and from Socrates Scholasticus in appendix D, which also gives the full text of Malalas's brief notice. There, too, will be found the texts of the relevant letters by Synesius. The question of the dates to be assigned to these, and to Synesius's life in general, is the subject of a recent authoritative study (Roques 1989). An earlier, and still useful, text is Crawford's (1901). My remarks on Theon's death are drawn from this source; with him I dismiss the suggestion that a Theotecnus, who does appear in the letters (see sections D.3 and D.8), is in fact Theon.

The canonical age for consecration I have taken from Crawford (1901). Roques (1989) gives the age as forty, but goes on to list numerous exceptions.

Likewise, Synesius does not refer to Epiphanius. This again inclines one to doubt that Hypatia had a brother of this name. If the earlier birth date for

Hypatia is accepted, then her astronomical collaboration with her father (occurring late in Theon's canon of astronomical works) would not only have postdated the dedication to Epiphanius, but also quite likely would have predated Synesius's studies in Alexandria. The two men thus need never have met, unless indeed Epiphanius had been a blood relative of Hypatia. The lack of reference thus militates against this latter hypothesis. The inscriptions referring to Epiphanius are discussed by many authors, but most accessibly by Knorr (1989) and by Toomer in his article on Theon in the *Dictionary of Scientific Biography*.

For the meaning of the word *teknon*, see that same article and also Liddell and Scott's *Greek Lexicon*, rev. ed. (Oxford: Clarendon, 1968). See this latter source also for the meanings of *thugater* and *pais*.

The Epiphanius entry in Damascius occurs under a heading linking Epiphanius with one Euprepius in Asmus (1911, 31) and Zintzen (1967, 75), which reproduces the *Suda* entry E2744. (See appendix D, section A.3.) The "thunder and lightning" Epiphanius is Epiphanios 11 in *Paulys Realencyclopädie*.

There has been one suggestion, which I discount, of an impact by Epiphanius on Hypatia's life. Socrates may perhaps be read as hinting at a perception that Hypatia practiced "magic" and John of Nikiu takes it for granted that she did. Hypatia's murderers, and also John of Nikiu, who defends and supports their actions, saw this as their justification. Were she linked to one who studied the mysteries of Osiris, their self-justification would naturally have been the greater. The suggestion of such a connection comes from Wernsdorf (1747/8) but, though imaginative, it is unsupported. Indeed, we may now argue against it. For had he known of any link, however tenuous, between Hypatia and the cult of Osiris, John of Nikiu would undoubtedly have alluded to it. Wernsdorf was, of course, unaware of John of Nikiu's account, whose discovery came later.

On Hypatia's education, refer to appendix D; on Theon's preeminence at the relevant time, see again Toomer's article on him in the *Dictionary of Scientific Biography*.

It will be noted that Socrates, who was much nearer to the events than was Damascius, is also the more explicit as to the nature of Hypatia's beauty. The qualities he attributes to her are quite compatible with her being an older woman and so lend some support to the earlier birth date discussed above.

The gloss on Damascius's sentence, the one damning both women and mathematicians, is quoted from Marrou (1964) who follows Tannery (1880). The translation of the sentence itself is my own from the Latin version of Photius in Migne's compilation (1857–1866). For a slightly different rendering, see appendix D, section A.4.

The belief that Hypatia never married is again reinforced by Synesius, who never asks her to greet her husband on his behalf. The point was first made by Kingsley in the preface to his novel and is reiterated by Crawford (1901).

I take this opportunity to point out that a belief that Hypatia visited Athens is based on a misunderstanding of the *Suda*. For details see, for example, Hoche (1860) or Dzielska (1995).

The subsequent quotations are all available in full context in appendix D. For Isidorus's dates see, for example, the relevant entry (Isidoros 17 in *Paulys Realencyclopädie*). Among those who try to reconcile the irreconcilable are Fabricius (1718), Toland ([1720] 1753), Halma (1822), and Richeson (1940).

# CHAPTER 6

For the different assessments of Hypatia's status, see the material in appendix D. The other women philosophers are all listed in *Paulys Realencyclopädie*, where Theanno is Theanno 5, Hipparchia is Hipparchia 1, Eudocia Palaeogina is Eudokia 2, and Asclepigenia is Asklepigenia 1. On Hipparchia, see also Diogenes Laertius's *Lives of Eminent Philosophers*, vol. 2, trans. R. D. Hicks (London: Heinemann, 1925), 99–103. Theanno, because she was a woman and associated with the mathematician Pythagoras, is sometimes seen as a woman mathematician, but there is no evidence of mathematical activity on her part. Very little is known of her. Asclepigenia is mentioned by Crawford (1901). Duckett (1972), Dzielska (1995), and Waithe (1987) give accounts of yet other women philosophers. For Pandrosion, see appendix B and its notes.

The quotations from Damascius are given in two different renderings in appendix D, section A. The ones quoted consistently throughout this chapter are those from appendix D, section A.1, Winifred Frost's direct translation from the *Suda*. Much of the relevant material from the *Suda* also occurs throughout Dzielska (1995); this is not, however, direct translation as it reaches us via a Polish intermediate. A translation of the main section of the *Suda* article has also been supplied by Reedy (1993). The alert reader will note slight differences between the various English renderings.

Rist (1965) ascribes a very precise significance to Hypatia's *tribon*, and this will be examined in chapter 8.

The quadrivium (the fourfold division of mathematical science) was so described first by Martianus Capella in the early fifth century and more definitively by Boethius in the sixth century. (See the entry in the 5th and 6th editions of *The Oxford Companion to English Literature*.) I am assuming that they were codifying a somewhat older tradition.

Although the Greeks saw the heavenly bodies as material, they held them to be composed of a different stuff from terrestrial matter. This latter comprised earth, air, fire, and water. Heavenly bodies were composed of "quintessence," a fifth and qualitatively different element. This explains some apparent anomalies in the quote from Synesius, which comes from his *De Dono Astrolabii*. For a very full account of the concept of quintessence in the ancient world, see the article "Quinta Essentia" in *Paulys Realency-clopädie*.

The quotation from Synesius itself cites an earlier source: the introduction to Ptolemy's *Almagest*: ". . . only mathematics can provide sure and unshakeable knowledge to its devotees, provided one approaches it rigorously. For its kind of proof proceeds by indisputable methods, namely arithmetic and geometry." See G. J. Toomer, *Ptolemy's Almagest* (London: Duckworth, 1984), p. 36.

For astronomical details, many books are available, for example, the one by Hoyle (*Nicolaus Copernicus: An Essay on His Life and Work* [London: Heinemann, 1973]) or R. M. Green's *Spherical Astronomy* (Cambridge University Press, 1985). On the question of the Nile flood, see the *Britannica*. Theon may have written a book on this latter subject; see Toomer's article on him in the *Dictionary of Scientific Biography*.

The "transit of Venus" and its observation from Tahiti was the prime purpose of Lieutenant James Cook's first voyage of exploration. The observation was designed to lead to increased accuracy in the determination of longitude.

The *Tetrabiblos* has proved something of an embarrassment to Ptolemy scholars. Toomer in his article on Ptolemy in the *Dictionary of Scientific Biography* regards it as an inferior work even when judged by the scientific canons of its day. The authoritative work on Greek astrology is A. Bouché-Leclercq's *L'Astrologie grecque* (Paris: Leroux, 1899). For the Christian view on astrology, see the *New Catholic Encyclopedia*.

We may note that John of Nikiu's disapproval of music finds a parallel in Socrates' distaste for dancing exhibitions (see chapter 7). Asmus (1911) notes an ancient belief that flute music in particular acted as a remedy against lovesickness. Zintzen (1967) suggests that the "tales of music" were a Christian calumny on Hypatia. If so, it was one that (the pagan) Damascius was concerned to refute, but which we see preserved by John of Nikiu.

The "menstrual napkin incident" was recounted in full detail and in English by Toland ([1720] 1753) and not again without recourse at some point to Greek until Waithe (1987) reprinted his version. There is also a full and sensible discussion in Dzielska (1995). (The practice of using foreign languages to hide potentially prurient material is due to Gibbon, whose *Autobiography* boasts: "My English text is chaste, and all licentious passages are left in the obscurity of a learned language.") The date of 1753 given for Toland ([1720] 1753) here and elsewhere is that of a (posthumous) second edition. Toland actually wrote in 1720. Bury ([1893] 1958) regards *this* story as a Christian calumny on Hypatia, but the facts would seem to be against him. Unless the passage is seen as an interpolation, and Asmus (1911) does not see it as such, it comes from the pagan historian Damascius, whose tone in any case strikes me as supportive. (Zintzen [1967], however, regards the passage as doubtful and the text as corrupt.) Nor do subsequent Christian commentators necessarily regard her action with disapproval. Migne (1857–1866, vol. 146, cols. 1105–1106, note 1) tells the tale (in Latin) but does so in the voice of a Roman Catholic cleric cheering with gusto from the sidelines as a dedicated virgin defends her status.

The actual details of the incident are obscure. The menstrual napkin can hardly have been *in situ*, although Bury ([1893] 1958) seems to have thought that it was. (His account could earn Hypatia a place in *The Guinness Book of Records* as history's first accredited female flasher!) Two different scenarios are more plausible. In one, the napkin, possibly that of menarche, would be routinely carried as a talisman, or more accurately a counterpart of Christian scapulas or medals—a symbol of a mode of life voluntarily adopted for spiritual benefit. Alternatively, she could have planned the young man's discomfiture. ("Next time he pesters me, I'll show him something!") Either way, her tactic in repulsing sexual harassment seems to have been effective.

The use in the cult of Artemis of menses preserved from the menarche and the healing powers attributed to such a talisman are mentioned by Asmus (1911).

The "unclean" nature of the vagina finds an echo in the Christian doctrine of the Virgin Birth, which, literally interpreted, implies that Jesus' birth did not occur normally via the birth canal, but miraculously. See the *New Catholic Encyclopedia*.

For the question of age at menarche, see J. M. Tanner, *Education and Physical Growth* (University of London Press, 1961). I have taken the earliest figures from Tanner and assumed them to have applied in the fourth century (for which, of course, we have little direct data)—that is, I am regarding the present earlier age at menarche as atypical of human history as a whole; such a view squares with the more theoretical aspects of Tanner's work. For the relative rarity of menstruation, see J. Delaney, M. J. Lupton, and E. Toth, *The Curse: A Cultural History of Menstruation*, rev. ed. (Urbana: University of Illinois, 1988), 16.

Wernsdorf (1747/8) has a much longer discussion than I give here on the

Christian Church's distrust of mathematics. He quotes inter alia from a law promulgated by Constantius: "No one may consult a soothsayer or a mathematician." He also cites edicts outlawing various types of music. For another extended discussion, see Wolf (1879, 34). The briefer account I give in the text is derived from Blunt (1874).

John of Nikiu dismisses Hypatia as a woman devoted to "magic, astrolabes and instruments of music." The astrolabe has thus become in his eyes an astrological, rather than an astronomical, device. Compare my later remarks on the inability of such a man to distinguish true mathematics from false.

There is one further suggestion of astrological activity on Theon's part. Malalas (see p. 186 of the English translation referred to in chapter 4) has him expounding, inter alia, the works of Hermes Trismegistus, a shadowy figure whose work was seen as combining astrology with aspects of Egyptian religion. Malalas's account is, however, so much at variance with other, more secure knowledge of Theon, that it is almost universally discounted or even ignored. Dzielska (1995) accepts this passage as true, but she seems to place far too great a reliance on Malalas generally, and to discount or lack acquaintance with much of the literature on Theon.

My summary of Synesius's theory of dreams owes a considerable debt to the outline given by Eliade (1987, vol. 9, 97–98). The translations quoted and paraphrased are from Duckett (1972).

Dzielska (1995) goes into some detail on the question of Synesius's involvement with Chaldean lore, with which he was certainly very familiar. However, familiarity is not the same thing as acceptance, and this is the conclusion that she finally draws.

# CHAPTER 7

The "secular versus ecclesiastical" debate may be understood in more detail than is pursued in the text by continuing the use of the Malaysian analogy. Much of the thrust of today's resurgent Islam (elsewhere as well as in Malaysia) is the strong component of Islamic thought that requires Islam to be embedded in a society whose rules, observances, and mores are all founded on and bound together by the precepts of the Qur'an. For many Muslims, Islam is incompletely realized if it is not embodied in a fully and avowedly Islamic society.

In the fifth century (and indeed for many centuries thereafter), a very similar philosophy pervaded Christian states. The conflicts being played out today in Islamic societies are the mirror of the disputes between the spiritual and the secular leaders of Christian societies back then. We must remember that the strife between Cyril and Orestes took place more than a millennium before the American Bill of Rights was enacted. Cyril's actions should, just like those of Orestes, Hypatia, and the other protagonists, be judged by the standards of his time: a time in which there *were* no agreed standards (which was of course the cause of much of the trouble). I judge Cyril harshly, however, because his continued veneration explicitly advances him as a model for Christians today.

The main thrust of the narrative as I tell it paraphrases Socrates. However, I have not hesitated to incorporate into it my own judgments and what may be viewed as my personal interpretations of events. This I do with a clear conscience here when in other parts of this book I avoid it. My justification is that the unadorned sources are all provided for the reader in appendix D. Furthermore, this aspect of the story is the one most widely available, and the sufficiently assiduous reader may consult other renderings.

Mueller (1987) gives a concise summary and Duckett (1972) a fuller account. I have found Duckett's fairly accessible version very useful, but the reader should be alert for a few sillinesses and a number of downright errors that mar an otherwise good piece of work. There are also numerous other tellings of the story (Baronius 1601; Bigoni 1886/7; Desmolets 1749; Dzielska 1995; Enfield 1791; Halma 1822; Hoche 1860; Lewis 1721; Meyer 1886; Richeson 1940; Schubert 1906; Tillemont 1709; Toland [1720] 1753; Waithe 1987; Wernsdorf 1747/8; Wolf 1879). Praechter also recounts the events in his article on Hypatia in *Paulys Realencyclopädie*.

Wernsdorf's is perhaps the most scholarly and careful defense of Cyril. Toland by contrast had a clear axe to grind and is violently critical of the sainted archbishop, but his scholarship, though wrong in places, was until very recently unrivaled in the English-speaking world. There is a full and balanced assessment of Cyril's possible guilt in Dzielska (1995), whose views accord quite closely with my own.

An imaginative reconstruction of Hypatia's death forms the climax of Kingsley's novel *Hypatia*. Schubert (1906) in particular aims to refute it, but I am here prescinding entirely from consideration of explicitly fictional reconstructions.

The destruction of the temple of Serapis is recounted by the ecclesiastical historians Sozomen (*Historia Ecclesiastica*, bk. VII, chap. 15) and Socrates Scholasticus (bk. V, chap. 16). Cyril's initiatives against the Novatians are recounted by Socrates Scholasticus (ibid., bk. VII, chap. 7). See Zenos (1891).

The arming of the Nitrian monks is recorded by Socrates—see the excerpt given in appendix D, section B. It is not clear quite what this "arming" consisted of, but the use of stones in the attempt on Orestes' life may indicate a body of slingsmen. A cohesive body of five hundred slingsmen, each carrying some dozen or so stones weighing, say, 50–100 grams each, would be a very considerable force indeed. Socrates states that Orestes' guards in large number fled, "fearing to be stoned to death." For the power of slingsmen in ancient warfare, see the article "The Sling as a Weapon" by M. Korfmann (*Scientific American* 229, no. 4 [October 1973]: 34–42). Nitria, incidentally, is a mountainous region near Alexandria.

Bury ([1893] 1958) notes that Orestes, as *civil* governor, would not have had control of the military. This was separate.

Zintzen (1967) erroneously describes Orestes as a pagan.

The gradual obliteration "by silence" of the true facts of "Saint" Ammonius's martyrdom was in fact *very* slow. Although his name is now no longer in the calendar of saints, it was still there in 1924, the publication date of Holweck's *Biographical Dictionary of the Saints*!

Zenos (1891) quotes a custom of settling differences between disputants by an oath of reconciliation administered on the person, or by invoking the name of a child, thus powerfully symbolizing the commitment of both parties to life and to all that is best in human nature. Cyril's use of the Gospels in his attempt at reconciliation with Orestes may have been an observance of this custom—the symbolism being all the more powerful in that the child here in question was the Christ child.

I have referred to the Peter who led the attack on Hypatia by the Latin name *Lector* rather than by its English equivalent "Reader" because I tend toward the view that Socrates is here employing an ecclesiastical title. Dzielska (1995) also inclines to this possibility, but it is not an opinion that all will share, indeed Lewis (1721), for whose discussion I have very little time, attempts explicitly to refute it. However, there are, below the grade of priesthood, a number of lesser orders of which most readers will be familiar with the rank of deacon and probably no others. Back then, the second-lowest of these orders was that of lector, or reader. A lector was given the task of reading passages from scripture during the celebration of Christian worship. (See the *New Catholic Encyclopedia*.)

There has been some speculation as to Peter the Lector's subsequent life. A number of letters by Saint Isidore of Pelusium, a contemporary monk, theologian, and master of the spiritual life, are addressed to a man of this name. They are rather general exhortations to virtue (one is headed "On the loveliness of virtue and the vileness of sin"). Tillemont (1709) sees Saint Isidore writing "as if to a man who had need of strong medicines to heal the injuries to his soul." The letters are also noted by others (Bigoni 1886/7; Desmolets 1749, and Hoche 1860) and are to be found in Migne (1857–1866, vol. 78). Whether the recipient was indeed the same man as Hypatia's principal murderer will probably never be known. The name "Peter" and the appellation "Lector" (as I have interpreted it) were hardly uncommon, even if we restrict the time to the early fifth century and the place to Alexandria and its environs. Isidore's correspondents include several other *Peters*.

Dzielska (1995) discusses at some length the suggestion that Isidore of Pelusium may have been a pupil of Hypatia's; the basis for this suggestion is an inferred friendship between Isidore and Synesius.

I have translated the Greek *ostrakois* as "roofing tiles" and so do Zenos (1891) and Dzielska (1995), although the word can refer to other sorts of tiles and can also mean "shells," specifically oyster shells. Either shells or (broken) tiles could have been used more as cutting implements, rather than for striking and battering, and such an account is often given. See, for example, Gibbon's in *Decline and Fall*. However, whatever the weapons and however they were used, the murder was singularly brutal and our revulsion no less merited.

The suggestion of bribery comes from Damascius (see appendix D, section A). In section A.1, I have followed Tannery (1880) in using Anthemius as the name of the allegedly corrupt official. The text actually names him as *Aidesios*, and considerable effort has been spent in finding an Aidesius with a suitable descendant to fit the bill. See the notes to appendix D, section A, below. Tannery's plausible suggestion is that the name "Aidesios" is the result of a mistranscription, as the handwritten versions of the Greek characters involved are easily confused.

Damascius attributes Hypatia's death directly to "plotting" by Cyril, but his is a less-detailed account than that of Socrates, which strikes the reader as more authoritative. It would not be unnatural for a pagan historian writing some hundred years or so after the event to fix the guilt on the Christian bishop of the day. Hesychius states that Hypatia's death was the result of spite over "her outstanding wisdom especially in matters of astronomy." This, too, seems simplistic, but it may conceal a reference to astrology. Rist (1965) thinks this possible, even if Hypatia herself did not indeed practice astrology. I have given my reasons in chapter 6 for thinking that she did not in fact do so, at least not in any but at most a very minor way. However, I do take seriously the possibility that a *charge* of astrology was used to justify the crime.

Philostorgius, who may have had Arian affiliations—see, for example, Dzielska (1995)—explicitly attributes Hypatia's murder to the "homöousians," that is, the orthodox Christians. This is the general feeling and it accords with the natural reading of both Socrates and Damascius. Toland ([1720] 1753) also makes great play with it, describing the orthodox Christians as "Athanasian Trinitarians." However, the terms "homöousian" and "homoiousian" are easily confused. The latter word does not refer to orthodox

Christians at all, but, by contrast, describes a branch of the Arian movement. See Blunt (1874). Thus, Mueller (1987) has it that Philostorgius is blaming the Arians; another such attempt to shift the guilt to the Arians is made by Desmolets (1749); see the notes to appendix D, section E. I have rejected this suggestion and the translation given in appendix D reflects this understanding.

The subsequent correspondence on the "parabolans" (or *parabolani*) was discovered as the result of diligent detective work by Baronius (1601); the story is retold by Tillemont (1709) and is referred to by Schubert (1906). Gibbon's *Decline and Fall* also contains a brief account of the matter. I assume along with many others that the parabolans, the monks of Nitria, and Hypatia's murderers were all the same group of people. This fits the canon of parsimony, but is not directly attested. Moreover, Dzielska (1995) demurs.

The assessment quoted on the matter of Cyril's guilt is from Canon W. Bright's *A History of the Church from the Edict of Milan, A.D. 313, to the Council of Chalcedon, A.D. 451* (Oxford: Parker, 1860), 274–75.

# CHAPTER 8

We have very little direct knowledge of the philosophy Hypatia espoused beyond the fact that it was Neoplatonist and that she lectured on Plato, Aristotle, and others. Even the circumstances of her teaching are disputed. Rist (1965) has her lecturing at public expense, but Évrard (1977) has her merely lecturing in public, a position with which Dzielska (1995) agrees. It all depends on how one translates the *Suda*; the English versions in appendix D, section A, follow the latter interpretation.

As for the philosophical content of her lectures, we have almost every conceivable suggestion being advanced by someone. F. Coppleston (*A History of Philosophy* [London: Search, 1946]) has her merely explicating the text of Plato and Aristotle, particularly the logical works (a suggestion I regard as unlikely). Rist (1965) minimizes the speculative (i.e., religious) elements and stresses perceived Cynic aspects. Lacombrade (1951, 1978) takes the opposite view. My own reasons for suggesting that Cynic elements played little role in

Hypatia's philosophy are given in the text. Dzielska (1995) likewise dismisses the suggestion, but on other grounds. In the main, I follow Bregman (1982), whose views are close to those of Lacombrade and not incompatible with those of Knorr (1989). See also Duckett (1972). I have not however pursued suggestions of Stoic influences, although they have a certain plausibility (the Stoics, like the Cynics, stressed renunciation, but were both more rational and less extreme—see, for example, the *Britannica*).

The apparent discrepancy between Damascius's two assessments of Hypatia may be due to the fact that he actually wrote not one but two lives (today concatenated) of his teacher, or else to the possibility that the earlier passage is not in fact by Damascius; see Zintzen (1967) and the discussion in the notes to appendix D, section A.3, below.

Synesius is the subject of a number of studies (Bregman 1982; Crawford 1901; Duckett 1972; Dzielska 1995; FitzGerald 1926; Gardner 1886; Lacombrade 1951, 1978; Marrou 1952, 1964; and Roques 1989). His published works are still with us and the influence of Hypatia on Synesius is direct and well attested. For this reason, I have relied heavily on the methodology of attributing Synesius's ideas, or at least a general sympathy with them, to Hypatia. This is also the approach adopted by Dzielska (1995), and indeed it seems the obvious way to go. More indirect approaches such as, for example, considering the views of Hierocles seem to me to be too far removed to admit. The reference to the "sacred" nature of geometry is from a letter not included in appendix D, but see Lacombrade (1951, 42).

The literary references in Synesius's writings are the subject of an extensive concordance in Crawford (1901), who, however, admits that it is unlikely to be complete. A brief statistical summary is given by FitzGerald (1926) and is cited by Rist (1965). A somewhat different approach (involving a computer search of vocabulary items) is briefly reported by Dzielska (1995); on this basis, she believes that Synesius *did* know the work of Iamblichus.

Theon's dissatisfaction with the quality of his students is discussed in the article on him in the *Dictionary of Scientific Biography*.

For the specifics of Synesius's letters to Hypatia, see appendix D, section D.

The religious views of Synesius and his conversion to Christianity are discussed by many authors. See the list above. However, by no means do all these authors agree. In fact, some authors believe Synesius to have been raised as a Christian—see Dzielska (1995) for an extended discussion of the matter. However Bregman (1982), Lacombrade (1951), and Marrou (1952) all have the account as I have here given it.

The quotation given in the text to show the mystical character of Synesius's Neoplatonism is from the *Dion* as quoted by Duckett (1972). However, my account of the *Dion* follows Bregman (1982) more than any other single writer. Other more general accounts of the effect of Neoplatonism on Christianity are given by the *New Catholic Encyclopedia* and by Eliade (1987). The collection in which Marrou's 1964 paper is published (*The Conflict between Paganism and Christianity in the Fourth Century*, ed. A. Momigliano [Oxford: Clarendon, 1963]) has a wealth of background material on the same and related matters.

The quotation from John's gospel is of course its opening sentence. The translation is that of Knox, and I choose it purely on the ground of personal preference.

On the question of "ensoulment," see the *New Catholic Encyclopedia*. Synesius actually covered himself somewhat. His stated view could be read as making ensoulment and conception simultaneous, which is in fact the opinion espoused by the Roman Church today. He also listed other doctrines (the end of the world and aspects—unspecified—of the Resurrection) with which he had difficulty. These, too, Theophilus must have overlooked. For more detail, see, for example, Duckett (1972).

The identification of "white-robed philosophers" as pagans and "dark-robed philosophers" as Christians I have taken from Crawford (1901), but it is widely accepted by later authors.

The suggestion that between them Synesius and Theophilus managed to protect Hypatia from Christian extremists is my own, but it seems to me to accommodate the facts of the matter very well. Not only does it make sense of the personalities involved and their relationships, but it could hardly fit the dates any better. The account given by Dzielska (1995) is less explicit, but may be said to follow the same lines. Furthermore, it notes (her p. 41) that both Theophilus and Hypatia were approached to intercede on behalf of the same person (one Nicaeus) in the same case; I take this information as corroborative. Many of the other authors previously cited also deal with the relations between Synesius and Theophilus, although they by no means all agree. For Synesius's dates, see Roques (1989). The epithet "the providence of others" comes from one of Synesius's letters; see appendix D, section D.5.

On Cynics, see the *New Catholic Encyclopedia* and Blunt (1874), inter alia. The main supporter of the thesis that Hypatia had strong Cynic tendencies is Rist (1965). Dzielska (1995) disagrees, as do I.

Both Marrou (1964) and Rist (1965) object to Kingsley's novel on the grounds of alleged sado-eroticism. Opinions will differ on such matters. Certainly there is the "purple passage," previously noted, that Marrou finds exceptionable. Rist, in the main, follows Marrou, but also (via a footnote) draws attention to other aspects of Kingsley's work that have attracted similar criticism. However, Kingsley's literary star has now well and truly waned, and so we may safely neglect this controversy.

# CHAPTER 9

## Section A

For this section, and for an overview of Hypatia's mathematics, see Deakin (1994). See also Knorr (1989), in particular his chapter 11.

## Section B

For background, see Toomer's article on Ptolemy in the *Dictionary of Scientific Biography*. The translation of Theon's inscription quoted is from

Heath (1938). Halma's work on the *Almagest* is the first of his publications (1821). Rome's major work was published in two parts (1936, 1943), but see also his earlier paper (1926). Rome proposed the view that Hypatia contributed substantially to Book III of Theon's Commentary on the Almagest. For an opposing view, see Cameron (1990).

The details of the long division techniques are given in more detail in appendix A, section A, but see also Knorr (1989).

The quotation on Theon's style is from Rome (1943). Its translation is my own.

## Section C

On Knorr's methodology, see Knorr (1989), Rome (1936, 1943), and, for a critique, Cameron (1990).

## Section D

For background, see the *Dictionary of Scientific Biography* under "Apollonius," and also the extensive treatment given by Heath (1921, vol. 2, 126–96). The discussion of Hypatia's possible involvement in Eutocius's Commentary comes from Knorr (1989).

## Section E

Again, see the relevant entries in the *Dictionary of Scientific Biography*. The modern editions of Theon's commentaries are Rome (1936, 1943), Mogenet and Tihon (1985), and Tihon (1978). The final suggestion advanced in the text is based on J. B. J. Delambre's *Histoire de l'Astronomie Ancienne*, vol. 1 (1817; repr., New York: Johnson, 1965), 317.

## Section F

For the older theory, see the main article on Diophantus in the *Dictionary of Scientific Biography*, Heath ([1885] 1964), and the brief account in Waithe

(1987). It is also summarized, critically but fairly, by Sesiano (1982, 71–75). This theory (along with other, earlier, views) is also discussed by Rashed (1975) and likewise dismissed.

More recent scholarship is far from unanimous for, when it comes to details, the two principal names associated with the new discoveries, Rashed and Sesiano, differ greatly and acrimoniously. They both accept that the Arabic text discovered is derived from the work of Diophantus and that the relevant books are Books IV–VII of his original thirteen. Beyond this little is agreed. Rashed and Sesiano differ violently on what parts of the work are to be assigned to Diophantus and which to commentators, possibly including Hypatia. They quarrel also over the mathematical significance of the various problems, as well as over very many technical details of translation.

The Arabic material has been printed in three separate editions. First is an Arabic version, edited by Rashed and published in Cairo in 1975. This has not been available to me, but Rashed's later French text (*Diophante: Les Arithmétiques,* vol. III, bk. IV; vol. IV, bks. V–VII [Paris: Société d'édition "Les belles lettres," 1984]) is relatively accessible. Sesiano's edition is listed in the annotated bibliography and is the one I have most relied upon.

My assignment of the verification steps (but not the final summaries) to Hypatia comes from Sesiano (1982). See in particular pp. 71–75 of his book.

There are many reviews of these important texts. Sesiano critically reviewed Rashed's original edition (*Isis* 68 [1977]: 627–30), and "found much therein to criticize" (Knorr). Sesiano's edition was reviewed by Knorr in a useful article, especially for the study of Hypatia's possible contribution; see *American Mathematical Monthly* 92 (1985): 150–54. (The "trivial mind" quotation is drawn from this source.) Another important review of this same work is that of J. P. Hogendijk (*Historia Mathematica* 12 [1985]: 82–85). In particular, this discussion explicitly and completely refutes the suggestion that Sesiano plagiarized Rashed. Such a suggestion seems to be implied in a very negative review of Sesiano's work by Rashed (*Mathematical Reviews* 85h:01006). This review was later and in part retracted by the editors of *Mathematical Reviews* as being unfair to Sesiano.

A paper in Russian by Izabella Bashmakova, Evgeni Slavutin, and Boris Rozenfel'd has not been available to me, but it is the subject of a brief descriptive notice in *Mathematical Reviews* (83m:01009). Rozenfel'd also reviewed Rashed's (1974/1975) preliminary account in *Mathematical Reviews* (56 [1978]: #37), making explicit for the first time the suggestion that it was Hypatia's work that was preserved in the Arabic.

This list of published discussions is by no means exhaustive, and indeed I am aware of further articles on the matter. The only other one that requires mention here, however, is Sesiano's account of the Arabic texts in the supplement to the *Dictionary of Scientific Biography*.

My own view is that, as far as the mathematical significance of the various problems is concerned, it is Sesiano who is more likely to be nearer the truth than Rashed, whose judgments strike me as somewhat anachronistic (see the further discussion in the notes to appendix A, section C). It is beyond my competence to assess other, more technical, questions, such as accuracy of Arabic translations and the like. Undoubtedly the last word is far from said in this vexed area of research.

## Section G

On the general question, see the relevant articles in the *Britannica*. For more specific detail, consult Neugebauer (1949), who considers the question of Theon's lost Commentary, and also the *Dictionary of Scientific Biography* under "Theon" for more discussion on the same matter. An excellent introduction to the astrolabe and its theory is J. D. North's article "The Astrolabe" (*Scientific American* 230, no. 1 [January 1974]: 96–106). For the theory of stereographic projection, see also the article on Ptolemy in the *Dictionary of Scientific Biography*. The relevant basic astronomical questions are covered by R. M. Green (*Spherical Astronomy* [Cambridge University Press, 1985]).

Neugebauer (1975) entertains the hypothesis that Theon's essay on the astrolabe was a late work and could have been preceded by Synesius's writings. This is unlikely to be compatible with the dates suggested in chapter 5. Admittedly Synesius produced his work on the astrolabe early in his career.

In (probably) 405, he said of *De Dono Astrolabii* that it "was produced long ago in my ambassadorial period." This would make it a work written during the years 399–402 if we accept Roques's dates; by no stretch of the imagination can it be dated to a year before 390, and it was probably later than that. We do not know the date of Theon's death, but the dates I have favored in chapter 5 make it probable that he was not alive in 390, or at least died shortly after this date. Dzielska (1995), however, has him living longer than this.

It may also be said that if Synesius was born around 370, then his "long ago" was essentially the estimate of a thirty-five-year-old man of a lapse of five years. An older man would perhaps have used different terms. This further inclines me to believe Roques's dates. Thus, I am even further inclined to discount Neugebauer's suggestion. On the hypothesis that Synesius wrote a longer monograph on the astrolabe (and possibly sent it also to Paeonius), see in particular Crawford(1901, 509).

## Section H

The fullest discussion of the hydroscope and its nature is that of Crawford (1901), whose conclusions have tended to be taken for granted by later writers. The identification of the instrument as a hydrometer is to be found in Fermat's *Œuvres,* vol. 1, ed. P. Tannery and C. Henry (Paris: Gauthier, 1891), 362–65.

For the suggestion that the hydroscope was in fact a urinometer, and the consequences of this interpretation for the diagnosis of Synesius's final illness, see Deakin and Hunter (1994). I would now dissent from one judgment in that paper and not credit Petau (an earlier editor of Synesius's letters, whose comments are reproduced in Migne [1857–1866]) with having got the matter right. I now agree with Crawford that the first correct identification was Fermat's, and that all subsequent correct identifications derive from his.

One of the strongest points in favor of the theory put forward by Deakin and Hunter (1994) is that their initial draft, written in ignorance of the revised dating by Roques (1989), used the medical evidence to revise the date of the relevant letter, from 402 (H. Druon, *Œuvres de Synésios* [Paris: Durand,

1878]; see table 2 above) to 413. The authors later learned that such a conclusion had already been reached independently by Roques (1989).

A different hypothesis is advanced by Dzielska (1995): that Synesius, in extremis, resorted to hydromancy and that this was the purpose of the hydroscope. Not only is this somewhat far-fetched, but it is at variance with her own assessment of Synesius's views on such matters. Dzielska (1995) seems consistently out of her depth on mathematical and scientific matters, and the suggestion by Deakin and Hunter (1994) would seem to have much more to recommend it.

### Section I

For more details, see again Knorr (1989), and again take note of the cautions expressed by Cameron (1990). However, one point perhaps deserves comment. *De Curvis Superficiebus* includes a formula for the volume of a sphere. It is not exact, but uses the approximation 22/7 for the mathematical constant $\pi$. $\pi$ is most simply defined as the area of a circle of unit radius. On the other hand, *Dimension of the Circle* shows how the value of $\pi$ can be computed to arbitrary accuracy by establishing a set of inequalities. The unit circle can be enclosed in a polygonal figure with $n$ sides; likewise another such figure can be inscribed inside the circle. Using polygons of 96 sides, Archimedes in fact established that $\pi$ is less than 22/7. It seems a little odd that a mathematician, familiar with both works, would not comment on the discrepancy.

# CHAPTER 10

For the estimate of Theon's abilities and importance, see the *Dictionary of Scientific Biography*.

Of the many who have uncritically (and perhaps sentimentally) seen Hypatia as a greater mathematician than her father, we may perhaps note J. Gow, *A Short History of Greek Mathematics* (1884; repr., New York: Chelsea, 1968), 312–13, and B. L. van der Waerden, *Science Awakening*, English translation by A. Dresden (Groningen: Noordhoff, 1954), 290.

The opposing view is implicit in the attention given in, for example, the *Dictionary of Scientific Biography* to Theon and the relative neglect of Hypatia. In that work, Toomer's article on Theon is detailed, scholarly, and authoritative. That on Hypatia, by contrast, is best forgotten. Similarly, several commentators (e.g., Druon, the editor of the French translation of Synesius's letters: *Œuvres de Synésios*, chap. 5) have suggested that Hypatia's importance has been exaggerated by the manner of her death.

We should be careful to note, however, that Hypatia's place in history is *not* solely dependent on her violent death. Hesychius's account includes material independent of that event, and indeed Flach (1882) regards the account of her death in the excerpt reproduced in the *Suda* as a likely later interpolation. Similarly with Damascius, where there is much material besides the record of Hypatia's murder. Furthermore, the entire corpus of Synesius's letters predates her death, as Synesius predeceased his teacher. His writings have been preserved for reasons quite unconnected with her slaying. Theon's inscription is likewise unconnected with his daughter's death and the manner of it. Thus, even if we dismiss all the other primary sources, we have a comparative wealth of material. Contrast Pandrosion, for whom we have (in essence) only a little more than the equivalent of Theon's inscription.

Although the authors who have, realistically, attempted to reconstruct Hypatia's contributions to mathematics have differed violently on almost every point of detail, there is a striking unanimity of overall assessment: to wit, that her contributions to mathematical knowledge itself were slight or nonexistent. She was not, in other words, a research mathematician—rather a popularizer and a pedagogue. However, this, as I hope I have made clear in the text, is not to denigrate her.

That Hypatia should make her major mathematical work the extension and continuation of a program initiated by her father is not at all surprising; they had after all collaborated on an edition of his Commentary on the *Almagest*.

On the selective preservation of textbook material, see G. J. Toomer's article: "Lost Greek Mathematical Works in Arabic Translation," *Mathematical Intelligencer* 6, no. 2 (1984): 32–38.

The nature of Hypatia's mathematical work is best explored by Knorr (1989), whose discussion is the fullest available. As noted previously, Knorr builds on Rome (1936, 1943), but Cameron (1990) disputes the methodology adopted in this discussion. See also Deakin (1994) and Sesiano (1982, 71–75). Halma (1822) also attempts such an analysis but I have tended to discount it. The only other author to attempt to address the question in any detail is Waithe (1987), whose article strikes me as somewhat ingenuous, and in places downright wrong. (Regrettably, too, Waithe was evidently unaware of the revolution brought about in Diophantus studies by the publication of the Arabic material.) The accounts of Hypatia's mathematics in Dzielska (1995) are best passed over. Even the most adulatory of these authors (Waithe and Halma), however, offer no evidence of research mathematics on Hypatia's part.

The suggestion that Hypatia taught Jews as well as Christians and pagans comes from Crawford (1901), who notes one "Abramius" among the circle of Synesius, and thus very likely a pupil of Hypatia.

The best account of mathematics outside the Roman Empire is to be found in G. G. Joseph's *The Crest of the Peacock: Non-European Roots of Mathematics* (London: Penguin, 1990).

# APPENDIX A

## Section A

The representation of numbers is discussed very fully by Heath (1921, chap. II). The accounts of the long division algorithms are taken from Knorr (1989), but see also Rome (1936, 1943) and J. B. J. Delambre's *Histoire de l'Astronomie Ancienne,* vol. 2 (1817; repr., New York: Johnson, 1965), pp. 576–77. Rome speculates that the computational technique was designed to be applied with the aid of an abacus. He reports on some experiments he himself conducted in this direction.

## Section B

The fullest readily accessible account of Apollonius's *Conics* is that in Heath (1921). The discussion in the *Dictionary of Scientific Biography* is also accurate and authoritative, and that of Knorr (1989) is very much to the point as it is more specialized to the job in hand. I have relied here particularly on Knorr (1989) and Heath (1921).

The use of coordinate representation is of course anachronistic, but as it is the language of modern mathematics, and is moreover so well adapted to the task at hand, it would be foolish not to employ it.

It should perhaps be pointed out that there is no need to take $x = 0$ as the intersecting plane in the oblique case; this is done for purposes of illustration only.

## Section C

In the main, my comments are drawn from Heath ([1885] 1964) and Sesiano (1982). The actual examples discussed in the text are so discussed in Heath ([1885] 1964). For a recent discussion of Fermat's Last Theorem, see, for example, A. van der Poorten's *Notes on Fermat's Last Theorem* (New York: Wiley-Interscience, 1996).

As an example of the mathematical content of the dispute between Sesiano (1982) and Rashed (1975), consider Problem 17 of Book VI. This seeks the solution (in rational numbers) of the equation $x^2 + x^4 + x^8 = y^2$ and, by means of the relatively obvious substitution, $y = x^4 + 1/2$ discovers the solution $x = 1/2$, $y = 9/16$.

Of this problem, Sesiano remarks (his p. 259) that it is "hardly less trivial than interpolated propositions." Rashed, however (in his review of Sesiano 1982, in *Mathematical Reviews* 85h:01009, cited above in chapter 9), notes that in the light of modern results the equation can have only finitely many solutions. He further states that the solution found by Diophantus (or else by some later scholiast) may indeed be unique and that it is not known yet whether or not this is the case. (This question has since been resolved; Joseph L. Wetherell has shown the solution to be unique. See *Manuscripta Mathematica* 100 [1999], 519–33: MR 2001g11098.)

To my mind, this is to forget that Diophantus was not greatly interested in such questions, and for this reason I judge the comment and others like it to be anachronistic. The *problem* is not, to our twenty-first-century eyes, trivial, but the *treatment* given to it is possibly deserving of this epithet.

Similar remarks apply to Problem 11 of Book VI, which we would write $x^3 + x^6 = y^2$ and to which "Diophantus" gives the solution $x = 1/2$, $y = 3/8$. This solution is now known to be unique, a point noted by both Sesiano and Rashed. However, Sesiano is inclined (in a somewhat inconclusive passage) to attribute the problem to a scholiast. The uniqueness of the solution depends on the fact that the equation (in positive integers) $n^2 - 1 = m^3$ has the unique solution $n = 3$, $m = 2$. This was certainly not known to Diophantus, and again it was not the sort of question to interest him. (The uniqueness was first shown by Leonhard Euler (1707–1783). See either P. Ribenboim's *13 Lectures on Fermat's Last Theorem* (New York: Springer, 1979), p. 236, which places this problem in the wider framework of the so-called Catalan Conjecture, or else Ribenboim's later and more specialized work, *Catalan's Conjecture* (Boston: Academic Press, 1994). Thus, to our eyes, the problem has great significance. The "Diophantus" solution is rather garbled at this point. It may be, as Sesiano seems to say, that it simply relies on the observation that 9 (=$3^2$) and 8 (=$2^3$) differ by one. Arithmetically, this is a piece of trivia and must have been discovered over and over again from time immemorial. It acquires its significance from the more modern uniqueness result, which was outside Diophantus's agenda.

Just once in his work does Diophantus allude to a negative result. In "VI".14 he has: "This equation we cannot solve because 15 is not the sum of two squares." See Heath ([1885] 1964, 70), who shows that the claim is immediate if we accept the unproved claim that 15 is *not* the sum of two (rational) squares. The proof of this prior proposition is more difficult. Nonetheless, I adhere to my view that such negative results lay outside the main thrust of Diophantus's agenda.

## Section D

For more detail, see the article by North ("The Astrolabe," *Scientific American* 230, no. 1 [January 1974]: 96–106) on which my discussion is based. (Note one minor error, however: the caption to the figure on his p. 100 places the hypothetical observer to which it applies at 40° north latitude; this should read 50°.) For a discussion of Hipparchus see Neugebauer (1949), who gives the passage from Synesius in which the attribution is made. Regrettably, rather too little is known of Hipparchus. Ptolemy's later work seems to have displaced his predecessor's. See the *Dictionary of Scientific Biography*. Again for general background see, for example, R. M. Green, *Spherical Astronomy* (Cambridge University Press, 1985).

North repeats the erroneous placing of Hipparchus at Alexandria, but otherwise his historical remarks are an interesting and accessible summary. Neugebauer, however, supplies much more detail on this aspect of the matter, while being extremely terse on mathematical and constructional detail, precisely where North's account is superb.

Neugebauer accepts the usual view that Synesius is discussing the plane astrolabe, as supposed in the text here. There is one problem passage, but it can be explained away.

The *rete* is so named from the Latin word for "net," an object to which it bears a fanciful resemblance. An alternative name was "spider," and this terminology was in fact employed by Synesius (see Neugebauer 1949).

That stereographic projection turns circles into circles is a powerful and perhaps unexpected result. It follows, of course, from the theory of conic sections that circles drawn on a sphere must project as ellipses (see section B above). That these ellipses turn out in this case to be in fact *circles* is the further and significant result.

The Tropic of Capricorn that usually furnished the edge of the astrolabe lies at latitude 23.5° South. Thus almucantars further from the horizon than (31+23.5)°, that is, 54.5°, would project as full circles in the climate for Alexandria; others as circular arcs.

# APPENDIX B

The article reprinted here first appeared in *Function* (a journal of school mathematics, published by Monash University) 16, pt. 3 (June 1992): 88–91. Since its original publication, Professor Treweek has died.

The two "means" may be interpreted in the following fashion. Let the two "extremes" be $a$ and $b$. Form $x$ ( $= b/a$). Next let $y$ be the cube root of $x$, and $z$ the square of $y$. That is to say $y = x^{1/3}$, $z = x^{2/3}$ in modern power notation. Then the two "means" are $ay$ and $az$. It should be pointed out that the process of "constructing" such cube roots cannot be carried out, in general and in finitely many steps, by use of ruler and compass (the classical Euclidean tools) alone. In particular, if $a = 1$ and $b = 2$, we reach the classic problem of the "duplication of the cube."

Pandrosion's construction (and the others with which it competed) allowed infinitely many steps. When (perforce) the procedure was halted, an approximation was produced. The more steps carried out, the better the approximation. If the approximation was continued indefinitely, the error involved in the halting could be made to become arbitrarily small.

The duplication of the cube was one of three such problems that have come down to us from antiquity: all are today known to be unsolvable, in the sense that no finite ruler and compass algorithm can be adduced for the general case. The other two are the trisection of the general angle and the "squaring of the circle"—that is, the ruler and compass construction of the constant $\pi$ from a given unit length. For more detail, see V. Katz, *A History of Mathematics: An Introduction* (New York: HarperCollins, 1993).

Aristaeus was a geometer, a somewhat older contemporary of Euclid. He is credited with researches into the properties of conic sections. Beyond these meager facts, little is known of him. Heron (or Hero) of Alexandria worked there in the first century CE and is better known for his contributions to physics than for his mathematical work, which, however, was also noteworthy. He is not the same person as the Heron who taught mathematics in Alexandria after Hypatia's death (and whose lectures failed to excite the youthful Proclus). John Philoponus taught in Alexandria in the sixth century CE and is best remembered as a philosopher. His work on the astrolabe, however, is one of several writings on this topic that are thought to derive from Theon's (now lost) commentary. See Neugebauer (1949). The mathematician Theodosius (as distinct from the emperors of that name) lived in the late second century BCE, and was a geometer and astronomer. His best-known work is the *Spherics*, a textbook on the geometry of the sphere.

Greek words inflect with case and also with gender. The vocative case is used when a person is being addressed. The vocative feminine is used when that person is female. In the case here in question, the feminine form has η, whereas the masculine has ε, the other form of the Greek vowel *e*.

Heath's (1921) book includes an account of Pappus's *Collection*. See also: F. Hultsch, *Pappi Alexandrini Collectionis quae supersunt*, 3 vols. (repr., Amsterdam: Hakkert, 1965); A. Jones, *Pappus of Alexandria: Book 7 of the "Collection,"* 2 vols. (New York: Springer, 1986); A. P. Treweek, "Pappus of Alexandria: The Manuscript Tradition of the *Collectio Mathematica*," *Scriptorium* 11 (1957): 195–233; P. Ver Eecke, *Pappus d'Alexandrie: La Collection Mathématique*, 2 vols. (Paris: Desclée, 1933); A. Rome, *Commentaires de Pappus et de Théon d'Alexandrie sur l'Almageste*, vol. 1 (Vatican City: Biblioteca Apostolica Vaticana, 1931). Rome (1936, 1943) are the later volumes of this last work.

That Pandrosion was a woman is mentioned by A. Jones in the work referenced in the paragraph above and subsequently in his article in *Companion Encyclopedia of the History and Philosophy of the Mathematical Sciences*, vol. 1 (London: Routledge, 1994), p. 65. Treweek independently arrived at the same conclusion but seems not to have published his information although his independence is vouched for by Berghout and Frost. The entry in *Paulys Realencyclopädie*, however, mentions doubts on Hultsch's account dating back to 1878.

Jones also mentions as a pre-Hypatian woman mathematician "a certain Ptolemais . . . quoted in Porphyry's commentary on Ptolemy's *Harmonics*." This last is Ptolemais 3 in *Paulys Realencyclopädie*, where she is described as a Pythagorean. Porphyry died in (probably) the early fourth century CE, and thus Ptolemais predates Pandrosion (and so also Hypatia). However, virtually nothing is known of her. Probably the brief paragraph in *Paulys Realencyclopädie* says all that there is to be said.

# APPENDIX C

For details of the Catherine legend, see Thurstone and Attwater (1956), Dzielska (1995), Farmer (1978), Holweck (1924), and the *New Catholic Encyclopedia*. Even the most credulous of these authorities (Holweck) finds little of historical value in the earliest accounts of her life. He suggests that the factual basis may lie in a story told by Eusebius of a noble Christian lady who resisted the advances of the emperor Maxentius, and lost her wealth. This lady was not, however, martyred and moreover seems to have been married. However, the date ascribed to these events (305) is that usually applied to Saint Catherine's martyrdom.

The suggestion that it is in fact Hypatia who is the model on which Saint Catherine is based occurs in the ninth edition of the *Britannica* (probably its first mention) and is repeated in the eleventh. It was subsequently adopted by others, notably Asmus (1907). Dzielska (1995) makes the parallel even closer by specifying that Catherine was proficient in "geometry, mathematics and astronomy."

For the extensive artistic tradition supported by the legend, see, for example, K. Künstler, *Ikonographie der Heiligen* (vol. 2 of *Ikonographie der Christlichen Kunst*) (Freiburg: Herder, 1926) or L. Réau, *Iconographie de l'art chrétien*, vol. 3 (Paris: Presses Universitaires de France, 1958). This latter lists 112 depictions, and the catalogue is far from exhaustive.

Dzielska (1995) quotes "a much-stained inscription" on a ruined church in Asia Minor dedicating it to "St. Hypatia Catherine"!

# APPENDIX D

## *Section A*

**1.** The English translation is by Winifred Frost from the Greek text in Adler ([1935] 1971). The interpolation "[one on]" before "the Canon of Astronomy" follows a suggestion of Tannery (1880), as does the name "Anthemius" (rather than "Aidesius") for the allegedly corrupt official. We have Hypatia "expounding in public" rather than holding a public position, although the sense of the translation has been disputed at this point. The second part of the entry (from the subheading down) contains two literary quotations. The first is from Homer's *Iliad* (bk. 21, l. 16); the second is a con-catenation of, first, a phrase from Hesiod (*Works and Days*, l. 187) and, second, one from *The Odyssey* (bk. 22, l. 40); however, there is probably reference also to the *Iliad* (bk. 16, l. 388).

Georgius was an Arian bishop appointed to the see of Alexandria by the emperor Constantius and killed in 361 under the reign of Julian the Apostate; Proterion was slain in somewhat similar circumstances in 457. See Dzielska (1995).

The translations "thrust" or "threw" of the feminine napkin are both possible. Zintzen (1967) regards the text as corrupt at this point, however.

It was once thought that the reference to Athens implied that Hypatia also taught there. This is no longer believed to be the case, but rather that such customs as reported here (from Alexandria) were also followed in Athens (see Hoche 1860).

As appears in (3) below, Asmus (1911) believed that some material is lost between the account of the menstrual napkin incident and the ensuing passage. The "descendant" who "paid the penalty" was identified by Tannery (1880) as the Western emperor Anthemius, grandson of Anthemius Regent and executed by the Suebian general Ricimer in 472 CE. Zintzen (1967), however, takes it that it was the emperor Theodosius II who is supposed to have taken the burden upon himself and whose descendent paid the penalty. See the notes to (3) below.

The final two paragraphs are not, of course, relevant to Hypatia, but are here included for completeness. The various persons named are the subject of notes by Zintzen (1967). Both he and Adler ([1935] 1971) regard the text of the final paragraph as corrupt.

Extensive passages from this entry appear throughout Dzielska (1995). These have reached their present form via a Polish intermediate. The reader may notice some minor differences between these, the present translation, and the excerpt in Reedy (1993), which is also direct.

**2**. Flach (1882) in his reconstruction of Hesychius's *Onomatologus* here follows the *Suda* exactly, but regards the account of Hypatia's death, which concludes the extract, as a likely later addition. This time Tannery's interpolation has not been included, as Flach shows no acquaintance with Tannery (1880).

**3**. The English translation is by Monty Wilkinson and me from the German text of Asmus (1911). Damascius's account is there reconstructed from the *Suda Lexicon* and from excerpts paraphrased by Photius. Photius's abridgment is to be found in Migne (1857–1866, vol. 103, cols. 1249–1310). The translation is somewhat free; witness, for example, the insertion of the word "bloodstained" as a description of the menstrual napkin—this word is nowhere in the original Greek, but it could be said to be implied. It should be noted that Asmus used an earlier edition of the *Suda* than Adler ([1935] 1971).

This first excerpt is to be found on pp. 31–33 of Asmus (1911). The italicized words in square brackets are interpolations by Asmus himself and are designed to supply continuity. A succession of dots indicates a presumed gap in the surviving text. The edition by Zintzen (1967) is arranged differently and makes no attempt at a continuous, coherent narrative; fragments from the *Suda* appear on the even-numbered pages, parts of Photius's abridgment on the odd. These excerpts are themselves numbered and the layout of the text indicates an order in which the various items are to be read. The overall production of an authentic continuous narrative is probably a vain hope in reality, given the state of the surviving text. Nonetheless, it makes for enhanced readability and for that reason Asmus's interpolated continuity is preserved here.

Zintzen (1967) has the relevant fragments as (in order) *100, *101, *102, 52, 103, *104, 53, *106. The asterisks indicate that Zintzen regards these passages as doubtfully attributed to Damascius. He also regards the text "she thrust [or threw]" (the menstrual napkin) as corrupted (on the basis of a misspelled word). The fragments 52 and 53 are those interpolated from Photius. Compare with the text given in (1) above. The short fragment *104 (interpolated along with 103 into *102) is omitted by Asmus, and also here. (It is yet another sentence on feminine napkins.)

Although Asmus notes the possible relationship between Hypatia and Epiphanius, the actual text appears to make Epiphanius a rather later figure; it is not at all assured that *this* Epiphanius is the same as the Epiphanius of Theon's dedications.

The "Persian mysteries" are the beliefs and practices surrounding the cult of Mithra, a pre-Zoroastrian sun god; the worship of Mithra, or Mithras, was encouraged in second- and third-century Rome, but later was actively discouraged as the emperors embraced Christianity. Osiris is the Egyptian god of fertility. For more on these, see, for example, the *Britannica*. Aion is less well known—he was a personification of eternity; see *Paulys Realency-clopädie* and compare the English word *eon*.

Asmus hedges his bets on the question of whether Hypatia's teaching was the result of public office or was merely conducted in public. The German can carry either meaning. The rendering given here is the best English compromise we could achieve.

The use of napkins in the marriage ceremony is related to the blood, not of menstruation, but of loss of virginity. The marriage became valid upon consummation. The goddess referred to is identified by Asmus as perhaps Isis, whom he sees as a goddess of love and fertility and the protectress of wifely virtues. Isis was an Egyptian deity, and can also be seen as the goddess of rightful succession; this would make the tradition here mentioned the counterpart of later such traditions in medieval Europe.

The "opposite sect" is supposed by Asmus to be orthodox Christianity, in contradistinction to Arianism. He suggests that a reference to the latter has been lost. Zintzen (1967) makes no such suggestion. Dzielska (1995) argues cogently that the other group are the supporters of Timothy, Cyril's defeated rival for the archiepiscopal succession on the death of Theophilus.

Asmus suggests that Aidesius was perhaps an uncle of Valentianus III, assassinated in 455. (This idea was first put forward by Valetius, an early editor of Photius, and was taken up by Toland [(1720) 1753].) Both Asmus and Bury ([1893] 1958) make Aidesius an envoy of Theodosius II, sent from Constantinople to investigate Hypatia's murder. There seems to be little evidence for this suggestion, nor do we know much else about this Aidesius. (He does not appear in *Paulys Realencyclopädie*.) Furthermore, the word *ekgonos* used here more naturally applies to a direct, rather than to a collateral, descendant; see Liddell and Scott's *Lexicon*. For these reasons, I prefer the amendment by Tannery (1880), used above in (1). However Zintzen (1967) believes Aidesius to have been Theodosius's envoy (but without needing to identify the descendant), and rejects Tannery's proposed amendment on the grounds that Anthemius's regency ceased in 414, that is, before Hypatia's death. Tannery, in fact, had anticipated this point, but supposed that Anthemius still retained great influence, de facto if not de jure.

**4.** This second passage is from p. 97 of Asmus (1911) and follows the same conventions. At one point, Asmus gives two different versions of what he believes to be the same sentence: one from the *Suda*, the other from Photius. Both Asmus and Zintzen (1967) continue with the remainder of the *Suda* passage, which I do not duplicate here. Zintzen has this passage as fragment 276, with Photian interpolations 163 and 164.

The view of Hypatia adopted here is much less sympathetic to Hypatia than that of (3). In particular, it takes a less favorable view of her (nonmathematical) philosophy. Zintzen (1967) regards this later passage as coming from a different work from the previous ones. (In other words, there were two versions of Damascius's *Life*.) The reader will note also that he also regards as doubtful the attribution of most of the earlier passages to Damascius himself. These may be the reasons for a discrepancy already discussed in chapters 5 and 8 above.

## Section B

**1**. This section and the next are held to be relevant to the Hypatia story, most directly because they relate the dispute between Orestes and Cyril. Hypatia was held to be responsible for the continuation of their feud. The excerpts given here are all from Zenos (1891). The sentence on Adamantus reads like an interpolation. The brackets indicating this are my own.

**2**. The Dioscorus mentioned at the start of the passage was a Monophysite. The word "kindled" at the end of the passage is given as "quenched" in the original. Clearly this is an error. The correction is almost universally accepted. The other passages in square brackets are my interpolations.

**3**. There is some doubt as to the precise nature of the weapons used in Hypatia's murder. See the notes to chapter 7 above. The word "considerable" is my elucidation of a passage whose meaning has reversed in today's English usage. A number of separate quotations in Dzielska (1995) present much of this material in a somewhat different rendering.

## Section C

The original was probably written in Greek, possibly with Coptic insertions. It was translated into Arabic and from there into Ethiopic. Only two rather imperfect, closely related, and very late manuscripts survive (both in Ethiopic), and no printing was undertaken until 1883. The brackets signal various different things (carefully differentiated by means of separate special symbols and footnotes by Charles ([1916] 1981?), whose translation I otherwise follow):

"her" is an interpolation by Charles,
"But he once . . . danger." is seen by Charles as a corrupt transcription,
"dancers" is Charles's correction of the original text,
"and he" is omitted by Charles as an incorrect interpolation,
"an edict" is an interpolation by Charles, as is "in the theatre",
"regarding" is Charles's correction of the original text,
"Now this man . . . edict." is continuity supplied by Charles,

"Nitria" is stated by Charles to be the region known in Coptic as *Pernôdj*,

"also" is an interpolation by Charles,

"patriarch" is my amendment—Charles has "chief magistrate" but notes that it is incorrect,

"And one . . . S. George." would seem, on stylistic grounds, to be an interpolation, although Charles does not flag it as such,

"lofty" is an interpolation by Charles,

"till they brought her" is thought by Charles to be a scholiast's interpolation.

### Section D

The text given here is drawn from FitzGerald (1926). For detail of the dates and of other editions, see table 2, chapter 4 notes, above. There is also much valuable material in Dzielska (1995), including extensive quotation in a different translation.

**1**. Toward the end of his life, many misfortunes befell Synesius. His children all predeceased him and his own health failed. He complained to several correspondents of their apparent neglect of him in this period.

**2**. For a discussion of the hydroscope and its purposes, see chapter 9, section H.

**3**. This is believed to be Synesius's very last letter, dictated from his deathbed. Roques (1989) dates this letter and the previous two to 413. With Crawford (1901), I discount the theory that Theotecnus is Theon.

**4**. This letter is obviously merely a fragment.

**5**. This is another late letter. The words "bereft me of my excellent sons" are a quotation from the *Iliad* (bk. 22, l. 44). The later words "Aforetime the Milesians . . . " are from Aristophanes' *Plutus*, l. 1002. The phrase "the providence of others" is sometimes rendered as "other men's blessings."

**6**. The opening words are a quotation from the *Iliad* (bk. 22, ll. 389–90).

The full quotation runs:

Even though there shall be utter forgetfulness of the dead in Hades
  I shall remember there my so dear companion.

The letter is also notable in that it is one of only two that actually *name* Hypatia.

**7.** This is a major letter, of great interest for the study of Synesius's thought, and thus, by derivation, Hypatia's. The two works he refers to *in extenso* are respectively the *Dion* and *On Dreams*. From the length of time he spends on them, he would seem to regard *Dion* as being the more important. Later thought has in essence reversed this judgment. *On Dreams* had a great medieval vogue. See again Eliade (1987, vol. 9, pp. 97–98). The third work referred to (briefly and at the very end of the letter) is *De Dono Astrolabii*.

Some references will need explanation for today's readers. More detail on each is to be found in, for example, *The Oxford Companion to Classical Literature*, 2nd ed. (Oxford University Press, 1985).

The white and the dark mantles refer respectively to the robes of pagan and Christian philosophers.

The *Cynegetics* is a book by Xenophon on the art of hunting. Hunting was a favorite pastime with Synesius.

The "Horn of Amalthea" is a reference to the legend that the nymph Amalthea nourished the infant Zeus with milk fed to him from a goat's horn. Zeus, in gratitude, gave the horn to her, after having first endowed it with the magical property of producing whatever she required. The Latin equivalent is *cornu copiae* and the English translation "horn of plenty." Crawford (1901) suggests that there is a literary reference to the author Diodorus Siculus (iv. 35).

Xenocrates was an early successor to Plato in the headship of the Athenian Academy. The prevailing attitude of the time was said to be "conservative" and this may explain the man's "stern appearance."

The "bull on my tongue" makes reference both to the author Theognis (*Paraenesis*, 815) and to Aeschylus (*Agamemnon*, 36). The "bull" is not, of course, the animal of that name. The word is used in its sense of "seal"— again not the animal of *that* name!

The extended reference to artistic conventions (hiding images of divinities within unworthy figures) is derived from Plato's *Symposium* (215A). FitzGerald (1926) quotes: "I say that he (Socrates) is exactly like the busts of Silenus which are set up in statuaries' shops, . . . and they are made open to the public, and have images of gods inside them." The reference is to Socrates' *daemon*, a demiurge beyond his own personality, properly so delimited. The iconographic tradition endures: the University of Melbourne has (above the north entrance to Wilson Hall) a twentieth-century depiction of the death of Socrates, showing his *daemon* inside him.

The passage following immediately upon this is an extended reference to Plato's *Republic* (509B). "Just as the sun furnishes to the objects of sight not only their capacity for being seen, but also their generation, growth, and nutrition, even so the objects of knowledge derive from the good not only their capacity for being known, but also their existence and their reality, though the good is not reality, and is on the other side of it, transcending it in power and majesty."

The reference to the competing claims of truth and friendship is taken from Aristotle (*Nicomachean Ethics*, i. 4, 1096a 16).

The recipient of *De Dono Astrolabii* was one Paeonius (see [12] below). Pentapolis was the then name for western Libya, Synesius's homeplace; see (6) above.

The extensive use of literary quotations and references that characterizes all Synesius's longer writings is evident here as well as in the three writings that were enclosed with it. He clearly expected Hypatia to follow and appreciate their provenance. This gives us excellent grounds to believe that Hypatia herself was very widely read.

**8**. This is one of the longest and most important of the letters, but most of it is not here relevant. Theodosius is not, of course, the emperor; and again Theotecnus is probably not Theon. It would seem that Synesius believed the last days of the month to be the more dangerous for sea travel.

**9**. This letter and (6) above were written from war-ravaged Pentapolis (western Libya) in 405/406. Synesius evidently greatly valued his contact with Hypatia and continued it even in times of great turmoil.

**10**. This relatively early letter (399) must have been written when Synesius's student days were still fresh in his memory. He has little time for the scholarly activities of Athens, preferring Alexandria, although the Museum must have been in decline (at very least) by the time Synesius undertook his studies. This is the other letter to mention Hypatia by name.

Hymettus is a mountain near Athens, famous both for its marble and for its honey. This latter was in short supply and very expensive, and thus most prized. (It should be remembered that honey was at this time the principal, almost the only, available sweetening agent.) Presumably the passage is meant to be interpreted allegorically. The teachers of Athens offer their pupils palatable nothings, whereas Hypatia imparted genuine wisdom and knowledge.

**11**. This, the very earliest of the letters here quoted, also recalls Synesius's student days, and its purpose is to keep alive a friendship from those times.

**12**. The description of Paeonius quoted here is from FitzGerald (1926). The criticism of FitzGerald's translation by Neugebauer (1949) refers explicitly to this source; however, he quotes this passage (including the part quoted in chapter 6) in its entirety and without amendment, whereas elsewhere he introduces changes. For other matters, see chapter 9, section G, and appendix A, section D.

## Section E

**1.** This is the translation given by Knorr (1989). The sense of the original has, however, been much disputed. Rome (1926) took it to mean that

Hypatia revised or edited Theon's work. This meaning is also that taken by Heath (1938). Knorr (1989) goes somewhat further by indicating which passages he believes to be by Hypatia herself. The understanding behind all this is that Theon, recognizing the superiority of Hypatia's work, suppressed his own earlier edition, in favor of one revised by his daughter.

Cameron (1990), however, demurs and suggests that Hypatia's role was much less; he takes the words "the edition" to refer to the interpolated text of Ptolemy's *Almagest* rather than to the Commentary itself, and thus sees Hypatia as merely assisting her father in the preparation of *his* commentary. A. Jones ("Later Greek and Byzantine Mathematics," in *Companion Encyclopedic of the History and Philosophy of the Mathematical Sciences*, vol. 1 [ed. I. Grattan-Guinness], p. 65) also demurs and has Hypatia merely proofreading Theon's work.

**2**. The translation is my own, from the Latin version in Migne (1857–1866). This differs from the original in one minor point, which I have ventured to correct. I am also adopting the suggestion that Philostorgius was an Arian, whereas the actual author of this summary (Photius) was orthodox. This explains his characterisation of Philostorgius as "ungodly," for blaming the orthodox party over Hypatia's death. Damascius and Socrates also place the blame in this quarter, in the former case especially so, if we take, with Asmus (1911), the view that a passage referring to the Arians has been lost. Mueller (1987), however, takes a different interpretation.

We may thus take Photius as implying that it was the Arians who killed Hypatia. Such a suggestion is made explicit by Desmolets (1749) and is taken up in Migne (1857–1866, vol. 67, col. 769) and by Valesius, an early editor of Socrates Scholasticus. Socrates names the church to which she was taken (see section B.3 above) as *Caesareum*. Desmolets (1749) claims this to be the name of an Arian church as does Valesius, but no one else follows them in this. The clearest and simplest interpretation is that the orthodox party (Cyril and his supporters) were the guilty ones. We may hypothesize that Photius, not being in sympathy with Philostorgius, has severely pruned the passage, which would otherwise have been the earliest of all accounts had it survived intact. That Photius did prune his sources most dratically can be

seen by comparing the left-hand pages (Photius) with the right (*Suda*, etc.) of
Zintzen (1967).

**3.** The translation is from Byzantina Australiensia 4, a translation of *The
Chronicle of John Malalas* by E. Jeffreys et al. (Melbourne: Australian Association for Byzantine Studies, 1986). Malalas writes some hundred and fifty
years after the event, and thus is likely to be less accurate than the more con-
temporaneous and detailed account of Socrates. He is, however, the only
author to comment on Hypatia's age. The sense has been disputed. Nor is his
source known. It should also be noted in this connection that Malalas's
account of Theon is most suspect, giving us a quite different idea of him than
that provided by other, more detailed and more reliable sources.

**4.** The translation is my own from the Latin version in Migne
(1857–1866). The date 406 is now accepted to be incorrect. That usually
quoted is 415, although some have argued for 416.

# ANNOTATED BIBLIOGRAPHY

Those works listed in the notes, but (being more important) not detailed there, are referenced and briefly described below. In cases where several editions exist, I used the one cited.

Adler, A., ed. *Suidae Lexicon*. In five volumes. Stuttgart: Teubner, 1971 (reprint of 1935 original). The standard edition of the *Suda*. The article on Hypatia is in volume 4 (pp. 644–46; entry Y166); that on Theon is in volume 2 (p. 702; entry Θ205).

Asmus, R. "Hypatia in Tradition und Dichtung." *Studien zur vergleichende Literatur-geschichte* 7 (1907): 11–44. A survey of writings about Hypatia, both historical and imaginative.

———. *Das Leben des Philosphen Isidoros von Damaskios aus Damaskos (Der Philosophischen Bibliothek, Bd. 125)*. Leipzig: Meiner, 1911. A reconstruction of one of the primary sources.

Baronius, C. *Annalium Ecclesiasticorum, Tomus Quintus*. Antwerp: Plantiniana, 1601. A monumental church history. The source of much subsequent scholarship. See pp. 382–84, 400.

Bigoni, G. "Ipazia Alessandrina Studio Storico." *Atti del R. ist. Veneto di scienze, lettere ed arti* 6 ser. 5 (1886/7): 397–437, 495–526, 681–710. A detailed biography, bypassing the mathematics.

Blunt, J. A. *A Dictionary of Sects, Heretics, Ecclesiastical Parties and Schools of Religious Thought*. London: Rivingtons, 1874. Somewhat opinionated, but nonetheless a useful reference on the subject matter of its title.

Bregman, J. *Synesius of Cyrene*. Berkeley: University of California Press, 1982. A study of Hypatia's best-known pupil.

Bury, J. B. *History of the Later Roman Empire*. Vol. 1: *From Arcadius to*

*Irene (395 A.D. to 800 A.D.)*. New York: Dover, 1958. Somewhat dated (the original appeared in 1893). Hypatia is briefly discussed on pp. 217–18.

Cameron, A. "Isidore of Miletus and Hypatia: On the Editing of Mathematical Texts." *Greek, Roman and Byzantine Studies* 31 (1990): 103–27. A questioning of the methodology adopted by Knorr (1989), this work argues to minimize the extent of Hypatia's collaboration with her father in his Commentary on the *Almagest*.

Charles, R. H., trans. *The Chronicle of John, c. 690 A.D., Coptic Bishop of Nikiu*. Amsterdam: APA-Philo, [1981?]. Reprint of a 1916 original. A translation of one of the primary sources.

Crawford, W. S. *Synesius the Hellene*. London: Rivington, 1901. A very full and thorough account of Synesius's life and thought.

Deakin, M. A. B. "Hypatia and Her Mathematics." *American Mathematical Monthly* 101 (1994): 234–43. A recent account by the author of this book, stressing Hypatia's status as a mathematician.

Deakin, M. A. B., and C. R. Hunter. "Synesios' 'Hydroscope.' " *Apeiron* 27 (1994): 39–43. A speculative hypothesis on the purpose of the "hydroscope."

Desmolets, P. *Continuation des Mémoires de litterature et d'histoire*. Paris: Nyon, 1749. See vol. 5, pt. 1, pp. 139–91. Some rather special pleading of the Christian (pro-Cyril) case. Dated 1727. Asmus (1907) attributes this passage not to Desmolets, but to a C.-P. Goujet.

*Dictionary of Scientific Biography*. Edited by C. C. Gillispie et al. New York: Scribner, 1970–present. In 18 volumes plus continuing supplements. A standard work of reference, generally of high quality but disappointing in its account of Hypatia.

Duckett, E. *Medieval Portraits from East and West*. London: Sidgwick and Jackson, 1972. Chapter 3 concerns Hypatia and Synesius. A few sillinesses and errors mar an otherwise fair account.

Dzielska, M. *Hypatia of Alexandria*. Vol. 8 of Revealing Antiquity. Translated by F. Lyra. Cambridge, MA: Harvard University Press, 1995. A recent book, translated from a Polish original. It deals with both life and legend and is for the most part scholarly and reliable, giving a picture not very different from that presented here. There is a brave attempt to discuss Hypatia's mathematics, but unfortunately this aspect is of extremely poor quality.

Eliade, M., ed. *The Encyclopedia of Religion*. In 16 volumes. New York: Macmillan, 1987. A standard and authoritative reference.

Enfield, W. *The History of Philosophy from the Earliest Times to the Beginning of the Present Century Drawn Up from Brucker's* Historia Critica Philosophiae, vol. 2. London: Johnson, 1791. See pp. 86–89, which essentially summarize source material.

Évrard, É. "A quel titre Hypatie enseigna-t-elle la philosophie?" *Revue des Études Grecques* 90 (1977): 69–74. A short note whose main thrust is that Hypatia did not hold down an official position.

Fabricius, I. A. *Bibliothecae Graecae*. Book V, chapter 22. Hamburg Edition, 1718, vol. 8. A once standard, now rare, book of reference. It lists and summarizes (in Latin) the primary and secondary sources then extant. In this edition, the Hypatia entry begins on p. 219. Volume 9, p. 718, gives a Latin translation of an abridged version of the *Suda* entry.

Farmer, D. H. *The Oxford Dictionary of Saints*. Oxford: Clarendon, 1978. A standard work of reference.

FitzGerald, A., ed. and trans. *The Letters of Synesius of Cyrene*. London: Oxford University Press, 1926. The standard English translation of Synesius's letters and including *De Dono Astrolabii*.

Flach, I. *Hesychii Milesii* Onomatologi *que supersunt cum prolegomenis edidit*. Leipzig: Teubner, 1882. A reconstruction of Hesychius's *Onomatologus*. Its relevant entry has been re-derived from the *Suda Lexicon*. The passage translated in appendix D is entry 814 (pp. 219–20).

Gardner, A. *Synesius of Cyrene, Philosopher and Bishop*. London: SPCK, 1886. A not particularly good popular study. Its best points are repeated by Crawford (1901).

Halma, N. R. *Commentaire de Théon d'Alexandrie sur le premier-[second] livre de la Composition de Ptolemée*. Paris: Merlon, 1821. An early, and poor-quality, edition of this work by Hypatia's father.

———. *Commentaire de Théon d'Alexandrie sur les tables manuelles astronomiques de Ptolemée, 1ère partie*. Paris: Merlon, 1822. An outdated edition, it includes discussion of Hypatia's life and death and attributes to her the authorship of Theon's *Small Commentary on the Handy Tables*. This conclusion is unlikely.

Heath, T. L. *Diophantus of Alexandria*. 2nd ed. 1885. Reprint, New York: Dover, 1964. The till recently standard work on Diophantus. Recent discoveries of Arabic material have caused many of its conclusions to need updating. The extant Greek material, however, is made authoritatively accessible in this work.

———. *A History of Greek Mathematics.* Oxford: Clarendon, 1921. Remains a major reference work, giving many details of the principal figures of the period. There is little on Hypatia herself as she was not a research mathematician and the work concentrates on these.

———. Review of *Commentaires de Pappus et de Theón d'Alexandrie sul l'Almageste, Livre 3 (Studi e Testi 106)*, by A. Rome. *Classical Review* 52 (1938): 40. Follows Rome in attributing the present version of Book III of Theon's Commentary on the *Almagest* to Hypatia.

Hoche, R. "Hypatia, die Tochter Theons." *Philologus* 15 (1860): 435–74. A major study, but (as is typical) bypassing detailed discussion of Hypatia's mathematics.

Holweck, F. G. *A Biographical Dictionary of the Saints.* St. Louis, MO: Herder, 1924. A work of reference on its subject. Less scholarly than others (Thurstone and Attwater 1956 or Farmer 1978), it nonetheless encapsulates Roman Christianity's popular attitudes rather better. Its author was domestic prelate to Pope Pius XI.

Knorr, W. R. *Textual Studies in Ancient and Medieval Geometry.* Boston: Birkhäuser, 1989. A most impressive account of its subject matter. Speculative but scholarly. Chapter 11 is devoted to Hypatia and attempts to discover what remains of her writing via a stylistic analysis of Book III of Theon's Commentary on the *Almagest.*

Lacombrade, C. *Synésios de Cyrène.* Paris: Société d'édition "Les Belles Lettres," 1951. See chapter III. This is a major attempt to reconstruct the influence of Hypatia on the Neoplatonic philosophy of Synesius.

———, ed. and trans. *Synésios de Cyrène: Tome 1, Hymnes.* Paris: Société d'édition "Les Belles Lettres," 1978. See in particular pp. xv–xxi of the introduction.

Lewis, T. *The History of Hypatia. A most Impudent School-Mistress of Alexandria: Murdered and torn to Pieces by the Populace. In Defence of Saint Cyril and the Alexandrian Clergy from the Aspersions of Mr. Toland.* London: Bickerton, 1721. The title describes the purpose and the attitude of the work. It is of poor quality. A partial transcription is available on the Internet via Landman's site as listed in the notes to chapter 1.

Marrou, H. I. "La 'conversion' de Synésios." *Revue des Études Grecques* 65 (1952): 474–84. A careful account of Synesius's thought, both pagan and

Christian. It occupies itself with a number of technical questions and then goes on to discuss the philosophical influences on Synesius, which would have reached him via Hypatia.

————. "Synesius of Cyrene and Alexandrian Neoplatonism." In *The Conflict between Paganism and Christianity in the Fourth Century*. Edited by A. Momigliano. Oxford: Clarendon, 1964. A study of Synesius as a figure intermediate between the Christian and the Neoplatonic "camps." The entire volume from which this study is drawn has a wealth of useful background material.

McCabe, J. "Hypatia." *Critic* 43 (1903): 267–72. Primarily an attack on Kingsley's novel, but scholarly and sensible.

Meyer, W. A. *Hypatia von Alexandria: Ein Beitrag zur Geschichte des Neuplatonismus*. Heidelberg: Weiss, 1886. A detailed and scholarly dissertation on Hypatia's life and philosophy.

Migne, J.-P., ed. *Patrologiae Graecae*. In 165 volumes. Paris: Migne, 1857–1866. A major compilation of Greek texts, with parallel Latin translations. It contains the majority of the primary sources.

Mogenet, J., and A. Tihon. *Le "Grand Commentaire" de Théon d'Alexandrie aux* Tables Faciles *de Ptolemée, Livre I (Studi e Testi* 315). Vatican City: Biblioteca Apostolica Vaticana, 1985. The standard edition of this work by Hypatia's father.

Mueller, I. "Hypatia." In *Women of Mathematics: A Biobibliographic Sourcebook*, edited by L. S. Grinstein and P. J. Campbell, 74–79. Westport, CT: Greenwood, 1987. The best accessible summary of all.

Neugebauer, O. "The Early History of the Astrolabe." *Isis* 40 (1949): 240–56. This is the place to look for more detail on the history of the astrolabe, in particular the contributions of Theon and Synesius.

————. *A History of Ancient Mathematical Astronomy*. Berlin: Springer, 1975. The author was one of the most respected historians of mathematics, particularly with regard to the ancient world. This text has a passage relevant to the astrolabe on p. 873, but there is other good background throughout.

*New Catholic Encyclopedia*. New York: McGraw-Hill, 1967. The most accessible account of the thinking of the Roman Church, on questions of both doctrine and history. Now available on the Web at http://www.newadvent.org/cathen/.

*Paulys Realencyclopädie der Classischen Alterum wissenschaft*. In 49 volumes.

Stuttgart: Druckenmuller, 1914. A standard work of reference. It comes also in a smaller version: *Der Kleine Pauly* (Stuttgart: Druckenmuller, 1967). The article on Hypatia in the larger version is excellent, although dated on some points. That in the smaller is simply a brief summary.

Penella, R. J. "When Was Hypatia Born?" *Historia* 33 (1984): 126–28. A careful sifting of all the evidence on the date of Hypatia's birth. The conclusion is that the date is most uncertain, but that the ca. 370 so commonly quoted should no longer be propagated.

Rashed, R. "Les travaux perdus de Diophante I, II." *Revue d'Histoire des Sciences* 27 (1974): 97–122; 28 (1975): 3–30. A brief account of the Arabic translations of lost works by Diophantus. The conclusions are controversial. Some authorities think that some of Hypatia's mathematical writing is preserved in the material here described.

Reedy, J. "The Life of Hypatia from *The Suda*." *Alexandria* 2 (1993): 57–58. Published by Phanes Press, Grand Rapids, MI. Also available on the Internet at http://cosmopolis.com/alexandria/hypatia-bio-suda.html. A translation into English of the main section of the *Suda* article on Hypatia.

Richeson, A. W. "Hypatia of Alexandria." *National Mathematics Magazine* 15 (1940): 74–82. A quite interesting and informative article on Hypatia; it is a little puzzling, however, in view of its target audience, that it devotes so little space to her mathematics.

Rist, J. M. "Hypatia." *Phoenix* 19 (1965): 214–25. A good and reasonably accessible account. However it argues the case for Hypatia's philosophy having strong Cynic affiliations—a view which is here discounted.

Rome, A. "Le troisième livre des commentaires sur l' 'Almageste' par Théon et Hypatie." *Annales de la société scientifique de Bruxelles* 46 (1926): 1–14. The first paper to advance the suggestion of textual analysis to reconstruct the mathematical contributions of Hypatia.

———. *Commentaires de Pappus et de Théon d'Alexandrie sur l'Almageste, Livre 2 (Studi e Testi* 72). Vatican City: Biblioteca Apostolica Vaticana, 1936. The definitive modern edition of this work by Hypatia's father.

———. *Commentaires de Pappus et de Théon d'Alexandrie sur l'Almageste, Livre 3 (Studi e Testi* 106). Vatican City: Biblioteca Apostolica Vaticana, 1943. A continuation of the above work.

Roques, D. *Études sur la correspondence de Synésios de Cyrène.* Brussels: Latomus, 1989. (Volume 205 of *Revue d'études latines.*) A most important and thorough study, giving in particular the most up-to-date chronology.

Schmidt, I. A. *Variorum Philosophicorum Decas*. Jena: Ohrlingius, 1691. The section (IV) on Hypatia is basically a rendering of source material.

Schubert, H. von. "Hypatia von Alexandria in Wahrheit und Dichtung." *Preussische Jahrbuch* 124 (1906): 42–60. Essentially a response to Kingsley's novel, and an attempt to refute its imputations.

Seeck, O. *Geschichte des Untergangs der antiken Welt, Bd.* 6. Darmstadt: Wissenschaft liche Buchgesellschaft, 1966. See pp. 78–79, 404–405. There is, in particular, an extensive discussion of the date of Hypatia's death.

Sesiano, J. *Books IV to VII of Diophantus'* Arithmetica. New York: Springer, 1982. See especially pp. 71–75. This is one of the available editions of this new material. The other two have been produced by Rashed, but this one is the most accessible, and arguably the best.

Sextus. *Sentences de Sextius: Philosophe Pythagoricien.* Translated by C.-P. Lasteyrie. Paris: Pagnerre, 1843. This edition includes a retelling of Hypatia's story, based on primary sources. See pp. 271–304.

Tannery, P. "L'article de Suidas sur Hypatie." *Annales de la Faculté des Lettres de Bordeaux* 2 (1880): 197–200. An analysis of the *Suda* entry on Hypatia. Much subsequent comment relies on this short note.

Thurstone, H. J., and D. Attwater. *Butler's Lives of the Saints.* London: Burns Oates, 1956. The standard reference on its subject.

Tihon, A. *Le "Petit Commentaire" de Théon d'Alexandrie aux Tables Faciles de Ptolemée, Livre I (Studi e Testi 282).* Vatican City: Biblioteca Apostolica Vaticana, 1978. Now the standard edition of this work by Hypatia's father.

Tillemont, L. S. Le Nain de. *Mémoires pour servir a l'Histoire Ecclesiastique des six premiers siecles.* Vol. 14. Paris: Robustel, 1709. A large and comprehensive ecclesiastical history. The treatment of Hypatia begins on p. 267 with an account of Cyril.

Toland, J. *Hypatia: or the history of a Most beautiful, most vertuous, most learned and every way accomplish'd Lady Who Was torn to pieces by the CLERGY of Alexandria, to gratify the Pride, Emulation and Cruelty of their ARCHBISHOP, commonly but undeservedly stiled St. CYRIL.* London: Cooper, Reeve and Simpson, 1753. The title gives the flavor, but the scholarship is impressive, if by modern standards dated. Until recently, the last major work in English; this edition is a reprint of a 1720 original. The work was also anthologized in Toland's *Tetradymus*.

Waithe, M. E. *A History of Women Philosophers*. Vol. 1: *Ancient Women Philosophers, 600 B.C.–500 A.D.* Dordrecht: Nijhoff, 1987. See chapter 9. This account, unlike most others, makes a considerable attempt to discuss Hypatia's mathematics. Regrettably that discussion is not very well informed; in particular it proceeds in ignorance of 1970s revision of Diophantus scholarship.

Wernsdorf, I. C. *Dissertatio Academica I–IV: De Hypatia Philosopha Alexandrina*. Witenberg: Officin Scholomachiana, 1747/8. The benchmark for subsequent scholarship. Its only defect is the besetting one of neglecting Hypatia's mathematics.

Wolf, S. *Hypatia, die Philosophin von Alexandrien: Ihr Leben, Wirken und Lebensende nach den Quellenschriften dargestellt*. Vienna: Hölder, 1879. An annotated guide to the primary sources.

Wolfius, J. C. *Mulierum Graecarum quae oratione prosa usae sunt fragmenta et elogia graece et latine cum vivorum doctorum notis et indicibus accedit catalogus foeminarum sapientia artibus scriptisque apud graecos romanos aliasque gentes olim illustrium curante*. Gottingen: Vandenhoek, 1739. The relevant passage begins on p. 72 and comprises Greek and Latin versions of the primary sources with footnotes.

Zenos, A. C. *The Ecclesiastical Histories of Sozomen and Socrates Scholasticus*. Oxford: Parker, 1891.

Zintzen, C. *Damascii Vitae Isidori Reliquiae*. Hildesheim: Olms, 1967. A more recent reconstruction than Ausmus's of Damascius's *Life* of his teacher.

# INDEX